SpringerBriefs in Computer Sci⟨

More information about this series at http://www.springer.com/series/10028

Jorge Cardoso · Ricardo Lopes
Geert Poels

Service Systems

Concepts, Modeling, and Programming

 Springer

Jorge Cardoso
Department of Informatics Engineering
University of Coimbra
Coimbra
Portugal

Geert Poels
Ghent University
Ghent
Belgium

Ricardo Lopes
University of Coimbra
Coimbra
Portugal

ISSN 2191-5768   ISSN 2191-5776   (electronic)
ISBN 978-3-319-10812-4   ISBN 978-3-319-10813-1   (eBook)
DOI 10.1007/978-3-319-10813-1

Library of Congress Control Number: 2014947695

Springer Cham Heidelberg New York Dordrecht London

Printed on acid-free paper

Springer is part of Springer Science+Business Media (www.springer.com)

Constructing a simple framework to model a complex intangible asset is an intricate undertaking

Jorge Cardoso

Services are an ever-increasing dominant sector in our economy—building a proper model to work with them is, thus, of utmost importance

Ricardo Lopes

The complexity of the world suggests a lower bound on the complexity of our systems— models are needed to simplify our world

Geert Poels

Preface

Paradigm Shift

Traditional business theories are based on the exchange of products, which usually are manufactured outputs. Through history, product transactions have been the base of world-wide economies. Nonetheless, in recent years, there is a growing trend in firms to transform or extend their manufacturing-based business models to service-based ones.

Economies are not centered around product exchange anymore. The award-winning article published by Stephen Vargo and Robert Lusch in 2004 points at a radical change, which places services at the center of exchange and products as mere distribution mechanisms for service provision. Is the key success of iPhone related to the product itself or also to the many services provided to consumers? Do people really "need" tires? Michelin's fleet management solution sells truck tires per kilometer driven.

This paradigm shift is especially visible in the information technology industry as it is a major provider of business services. As a result, the interest on services has grown rapidly and it has originated an emerging body of knowledge coined *Service Science*, which involves the cooperation of several scientific areas such as information systems, economy, sociology, and management. According to the literature, Service Science combines organization and human understanding with business and technological understanding to categorize and explain the many types of service systems that exist as well as how service systems interact and evolve to co-create value.

One discipline explored by this book is service systems. It targets to study complex service systems that aggregate and combine business, people, resources, and technologies with the objective of providing an added value to consumers.

Service Systems

The *service systems* discipline is still in its infancy and there is a large potential for new developments and research in this area. End-to-end service methodologies and frameworks, service architectures, service consumer interfaces, service models, and service languages will contribute in a significant way to the advancements already made by the academia and industry.

While Service Science, and in particular the field of service systems, encompasses several areas, this book provides a contribution by proposing a simple, yet comprehensible, model to capture the essence of service systems.

Intended Audience

The intended audience of this book is twofold. For researchers, teachers, and students who want to learn about this new emerging science, this book provides an overview of the core aspects of service systems. It is aimed at students of business, information systems (IS), and information technology (IT) management studying the field of services. It also targets business and IS/IT practitioners, especially those who are looking for better ways to describe, model, and communicate services.

Book Structure

This book is structured as follows.

- Chapter 1 introduces the field of services, its relevance for society, and the motivation for writing this book. It explains the importance of modeling service systems from what we call a white-box perspective (i.e., internal aspects of services are modeled). As with any scientific discipline, it presents a list of definitions to enable the reader to better understand the context and concepts of this work.
- Chapter 2 presents several theories from different disciplines that provide a comprehensive conceptual view on services (e.g., Service-Dominant Logic and Unified Services Theory). The goal is to construct an inter-disciplinary knowledge base that can be used for selecting concepts to propose a service system model adhering to a white-box perspective.
- Chapter 3 looks into the knowledge base developed, identifies the most relevant concepts, and proposes a service system model called Linked Service System for the Unified Service Description Language (LSS-USDL). Its name captures one of the underlying objectives of this research, to develop a model which could interface with USDL, a black-box service description language which only captures the interface (boundary) of service systems.

- Chapter 4 explains how a real service system can be modeled with LSS-USDL using semantic web languages, how it can be accessed and queried programmatically, and how it can be annotated with background knowledge. To be pragmatic, we model the Incident Management service from the Information Technology Infrastructure Library (ITIL), a set of best practices for IT service management.
- Chapter 5 presents a web-based tool that has been developed to ease the modeling of service systems and their translation to other service languages. The chapter explains how to use the tool to model three different use cases, which have been comprehensively described in the service literature: express mail delivery, bookstore kiosk, and photo sharing webapp.
- Finally, Chapter 6 presents our conclusions, a summary of findings, and implications of this work for service-oriented economies.

Dresden and Karlsruhe, Germany, July 2014   Jorge Cardoso
Brussels, Belgium   Ricardo Lopes
Gent, Belgium   Geert Poels

Contents

About the Authors

 **Jorge Cardoso** joined the Information System Group at the University of Coimbra in 2009. In 2013 and 2014, he was a Guest Professor at the Karlsruhe Institute of Technology (KIT) and a Senior Research Fellow at the Technical University of Dresden (TU Dresden), respectively. Previously, he worked for major companies such as SAP Research (Germany) on the Internet of Services; the Boeing Company in Seattle (USA) on Enterprise Application Integration; and at the CCG/ZGDV on Computer Supported Cooperative Work. He has a Ph.D. in Computer Science from the University of Georgia (USA). He is the Vice- Chair of the Semantic Keyword-based Search on Structured Data Sources COST Action, a EU research network bringing together more than 70 researchers from 26 countries. His current interests include service network analysis on the web and cloud computing management using theories and technologies from the fields of semantic web, network science, linked data, and Linked USDL.

 **Ricardo Lopes** is an analyst developer currently working in Brussels, Belgium. He has a Master's degree in Computer Science (2013) from the University of Coimbra, Portugal. His research focused on Semantic Web and Information Systems, and explored service system modeling using computer-readable formats. His experience working with different service systems includes work in fields such as media content delivery, industrial property portfolio management, and international telecommunications infrastructures. He enjoys working on challenging side-projects in his spare time; attending MOOCs on Computer Science and

entrepreneurship; competing in national and international Judo tournaments; and collaborating with children from pathological families and teaching them English as a volunteer in Poland.

 **Geert Poels** is educated as Master of Science in Business Engineering (Limburg Business School), Master of Science in Informatics (KULeuven), and Doctor in Applied Economic Sciences (KULeuven). He is a full-time Professor of Management Information Systems and member of the professorial staff of the Faculty of Economics and Business Administration, Ghent University. His main functions are chairman of the Faculty Scientific Research Committee, faculty representative in the University Research Council, and head of the Business Informatics Research Group UGentMIS (http://www.mis.ugent.be). He is an academic member of the UGent Center for Service Intelligence (http://www.centerforserviceintelligence.org) and is a promoter of the UGent research Consortium Innovation and all inclusive Growth (http://www.ugent.be/innovation-growth/en). His main research domains are Conceptual Modeling, Business Modeling, Business Process Management, Enterprise Architecture and Service Science.

Chapter 1
White-Box Service Systems

This chapter motivates for the importance of the research field of services for society. While various streams of scientific developments have been previously conducted, it introduces the concept of white-box service system modeling as an approach to model the internal aspects or elements of service systems. The end of the chapter provides an explanation for the structure and content of this book, which is self-contained and comprehensive.

1.1 Service-Based Societies

We live in a society of services. Although the *service sector* was initially considered a residual economic category, next to the agriculture and manufacturing sectors [1], in the last three decades it has grown to become the largest part of most industrialized economies [2]. Nowadays, it contributes to around 70 % of the total GDP[1] of Western Europe's economies [3]. It is by far the strongest economic growth driver in the world.

The term *service* was first used in the 1930s by the U.S. Department of Commerce's Standard Industrial Classification to denote the residual economic activities that did not fit into agriculture and manufacturing categories [4]. Services were called "unproductive labour" because their output did not result in physical goods, contrasting with agriculture and manufacturing, which were therefore called "productive labour" [5].

Traditional business theories are based on the exchange of products, which usually are manufactured outputs. Throughout history, product transactions have been the base of world-wide economies. Nonetheless, in recent years there is a growing trend in firms to transform or extend their manufacturing-based business models into service-based ones (this shift is often called Product-Service (P-S) transition or *servitization*).

Economies are not centered around product exchange anymore. The award-winning article published by Stephen Vargo and Robert Lusch in 2004, *Evolving*

---

[1] Gross Domestic Product.

© The Author(s) 2014
J. Cardoso et al., *Service Systems*,
SpringerBriefs in Computer Science, DOI 10.1007/978-3-319-10813-1_1

to a new dominant logic for marketing [6], points at a radical change which places services at the center of exchange and products as mere distribution mechanisms for service provision. Rolls-Royce sells "power-by-the-hour" (the service), instead of selling aero engines (the physical product). The customer buys the power the engine delivers and Rolls-Royce provides all of the support to ensure that aero engines can continue to deliver power.

Due to the service sector's growth, society shifted from a Goods-Dominant (GD) logic to a Service-Dominant (SD) logic, focusing on the creation of value rather than on the exchange of goods [7].

This paradigm shift requires new forms to capture, conceptualize, and formalize service systems so that they can be studied, analyzed, and improved.

1.2 Service Research Fields

Research on services has been approached from different directions, although some strands are more mature than others. This section provides an overview of the main contributions.

1.2.1 Technical Perspective

From a *technical perspective* there is a lot of work done regarding the description of software-based services, the description of service-based architectures, and service composition into higher-level business processes [8].

The interfaces of the popular web services have long been described using WSDL[2] (Web Service Description Language), a machine-readable format that allows systems to find out how to perform invocations and what results to expect. Later efforts focused on adding semantics to those descriptions, giving rise to initiatives such as SAWSDL, OWL-S, and WSMO [9]. It became possible to account for domain knowledge and not just technical syntax.

Standards for the organization and behavior of registries (in essence, catalogs of available services) also emerged, notably UDDI, which, again, was later complemented by semantic extensions or variants that enabled the search of services by business goals and not just strictly by the service name. Several other standards, collectively known as the WS-* family, addressed issues such as policy, security, reliability, among others.

The shift from silo applications to pools of services, that could be recombined as needed, called for efforts to describe service-oriented architectures (SOA). SoaML [10] is such an initiative for the model-driven software engineering of services. It addresses, for instance, service requirements, dependencies, functional

---

[2] http://www.w3.org/TR/wsdl.

capabilities, policies for use and provision, partitioning, or constraints. Soon the need for a Reference Model for Service Oriented Architecture was felt, and SOA-RM was created [11]. SOA Ontology [12] is an alternative, in the form of ontology. Along the lines of SOA-RM, there is also the Reference Ontology for Semantic Service Oriented Architectures (RO-SOA) [13]. Orchestrating or choreographing services to achieve the end goal of a business process has been the focus of initiatives such as BPEL, BPMN, or WS-CDL [14].

All these efforts show the considerable progress that has been done so far in service-orientation from a technical point of view.

1.2.2 Business Perspective

From a *business perspective*, the most notable effort to represent and reason about business models, services, and value networks was the e^3 family of ontologies, which included the e^3service and e^3value ontologies [15]. These initiatives constituted perhaps the most evolved suite able to reason about services and value networks from an economic perspective. The research has, however, not been much concerned with the computational and operational perspectives covering the actual enactment or interaction with services, nor with the technical issues related to enabling a web-scale deployment and adoption of these solutions.

Complementary work in this area is GoodRelations [16] (GR), which focused precisely on this last concern by introducing a vocabulary to describe products and services in a structured way so that, for example, web searches and comparisons could be more easily and systematically done by customers. Nonetheless, although GR originally aimed to support both services and products, in practice it has mostly been centered on products to the detriment of its coverage for modeling services.

1.2.3 Multiple Perspectives

Linked USDL (Unified Service Description Language) [17] was developed to fill an existing gap in service descriptions by proposing a specification language, which enabled the unified formalization of business, operational, and technical aspects. It takes a *multi-perspective* approach. The goal was to propose a language for describing business, software, or real-world services using computer-understandable specifications to make them tradable on the web [18].

Linked USDL takes the form of a normalized schema which is an approach used in many fields to facilitate the exchange of data and integration of information systems. For example, online social networks rely on FOAF[3] to describe people and relationships; computer systems use WSDL to describe distributed software-based services;

---

[3] http://www.foaf-project.org/.

eCl@ss is used to describe products; and business-to-business systems use ebXML[4] to describe transactions, orders, and invoices. Adding to these existing standards, Linked USDL describes services in a comprehensive way by providing a business or commercial envelope around services. Therefore, Linked USDL is seen has one of the foundational technologies for setting up emerging infrastructures for the Future Internet, web service ecosystems, and a web of services [19].

1.3 The "Transparency" of Services

Service modeling approaches can be described and classified according to the degree to which their internal and external elements of service systems are visible and modifiable to the outside world. The visibility of a service can be object of study from an external and internal perspective. Modifiability can be studied from an internal perspective. These two important variables, visibility and modifiability, have their origin in software engineering.

1.3.1 A Practical Example

Imagine that a consumer needs to interact with a particular service. For example, a service that calculates and prepares a tax return form for the fiscal year. The service is housed in a black box and has an interface with buttons, form fields, and status fields on the outside that allow consumers to download forms, upload forms, pay for the use of the service, and to check the status of the forms submitted. Consumers can only interact with the service without opening the *black box* and cannot see beyond its surface. It is only possible to see how the service works by pressing the buttons (inputs), filling form fields (inputs), and seeing what happens to the status fields (outputs or outcomes). The service takes certain inputs and produces outputs in response to the inputs. Perhaps because we do not know, or are not interested, or cannot afford extra time to understand, we make a deliberate decision not to consider what happens inside the black box that presents the system. The internal structure, in this case, is not considered or analyzed. A service that exhibits this behavior is termed a black-box service (Fig. 1.1).

On the other hand, a service can also enable consumers to see and modify its internal elements. Consumers can potentially explore a service internally and also explore its subparts. Internal elements can be composed of business process models, people, business rules, infrastructure, IT, and security aspects, which are involved during service provision. By analogy, services that exhibit this behavior are called *white-box* service. In this situation, it is possible to look inside the white box and try

---

[4] http://www.ebxml.org/.

Fig. 1.1 The transparency of services

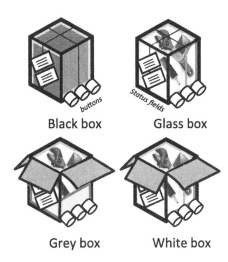

Black box Glass box

Grey box White box

to identify some of the elements that occur in the service, analyze them, and represent them with a series of models.

It should be noted, though, that it may happen that white-box services are composed at some point by black boxes. It is never possible to describe all the details of all the elements of a service. It is possible to go gradually into further depth in the service (which can be seen as having an element tree structure), providing more detail about its elements. As a greater level of detail is achieved, it is possible to find certain black boxes which we do not wish to, or cannot, consider in more detail. If that were not the case, the models of the service under study would end up being as complex as the original real-world service, and therefore would deliver little value for the purposes of service modeling.

1.3.2 Transparency Classification

With respect to visibility and modifiability, four main types of service modeling approaches can be identified (Fig. 1.2): *black box*, *glass box*, *grey box*, and *white box*. For all these types, interfaces are visible externally. If a service is a black box, it is not possible to modify or see its internal elements: it is used as-is. White-box service internal elements can be modified, even though this does not need to always happen. The term glass-box service means that a service has a white-box visibility but a black-box modifiability. A grey box derives from a white box for which only partial elements are visible and modifiable.

Black-Box Service A black-box approach allows describing a service with interface information that is externally visible to consumers. Nonetheless, the internal details

Fig. 1.2 Service
transparency classification

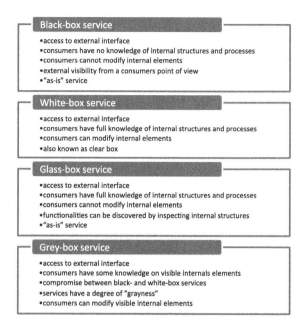

of services are hidden. The black box implies that a service is used without seeing, knowing, or being able to modify any of its internal elements. The service provides an interface that contains all the information needed for its utilization. Therefore, it is not possible to make any assumptions about the internal behavior, governing rules, business processes, or state of a service. The implementation is hidden and cannot be modified by the consumer. On the other hand, the implementation of its internal elements can be changed by the provider without any effects on consumers.

White-Box Service A white-box approach is at the opposite extreme of a black-box one. It allows to completely expose service internal elements to consumers, beside exposing its external interface. With respect to the interface, white-box services have the same characteristics as black-box services. On the other hand, with white-box services, consumers are allowed to "peek" inside the service and modify internal structures and processes. The term "clear box" is also used in the field of software testing to describe this behavior.

Glass-Box Service The term glass-box service classifies services that are used "as-is", like black-box services, but with internal elements that can be seen from the outside. Nonetheless, internal elements cannot be modified. This gives consumers information about how a service works without the ability to modify it. This internal visibility can be crucial for understanding how certain operations are carried out and finding the rules that govern a service.

Grey-Box Service When a service is viewed as a grey box, consumers have access to information that describes only part of its internals. Depending on the incidence degree of the "grayness", a grey-box service can provide different levels of exposure of the service internal elements to consumers. They can see and modify the internal parts which were explicitly exposed by providers.

1.3.3 Benefits and Limitations

Since the black-box view has limitations when it is necessary to discuss aspects of a service that do not appear in the interface description (for example, aspects related to the behavior of a service), this approach may not be always suitable for service system modeling, especially when consumers need to fully understand services. The approach falls down when a service needs to interact with third parties during execution since these interactions are not made visible to consumers. For example, when a front-end service has a back-end process representing its execution, the interactions with third parties expressed in the process are an integral part of the service. However, the black-box approach has positive aspects since it allows developing highly modular services and service compositions (i.e., business process models). As a consequence, any original service can be replaced with an alternative service as long as it has an equivalent interface.

White-box and glass-box services may in some cases be undesirable approaches since a consumer should be able to understand a service without being overwhelmed with the full complexity of services' internal structures, processes, and implementations. This high degree of internal visibility may lead to dependencies on certain implementation details which become fatal when the internal elements of services are changed. Unfortunately, giving consumers detailed information about a service's internal elements is often a compensation of nonexistent or insufficient documentation. While white and glass boxes enable defining exactly what a service does, and how it does it, they may in some cases be over-specified. On the other hand, this internal visibility can be crucial for understanding how certain operations are carried out. It may also give consumers confidence from being able to see inside a service and capture how it works. The observable internal elements may, for example, be state variables or interaction patterns. A suitable description should provide to consumers only the required information to understand a service, but no more than needed.

1.4 White-Box Modeling

As explained in Sect. 1.2.3, one of the goals of the Linked USDL and USDL family was to provide service description languages for managers to formalize their organization's services in a common, uniform format. However, USDL is limited to the description of a service from a black-box perspective, so a complete service system representation is not possible. Figure 1.3 illustrates this limitation. In other words, USDL views a service as a black-box and internal details are not modeled. For example, while the characterization of the provider, the technical interfaces to

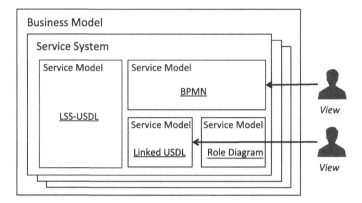

Fig. 1.3 Diagram explaining the relationships between business models, service systems, service models, service instances, and service descriptions

access the system, and the price of the service are all defined, no information is given about the roles and skills of the people which need to be involved, the physical and information resources required, or the physical location where activities occur. A white-box approach would enable to model in detail these information describing how a service works internally.

A model that could formalize and describe a service system's operations would result in many benefits, such as:

Transparency.   A white-box description lets stakeholders to better understand how service systems work. In many situations, *transparency* increases organizations' credibility, sustainability, and enables governments to clarify how taxpayers' money is spent. Recent movements such as Open Data [20] and Open Innovation [21] claim for a greater level of transparency. Business regulations, such as Basel and Sarbanes-Oxley, which define a "pillar" for how a business should function, can also benefit from making their services more transparent to managers.

Analysis.   Only after modeling a complete service system it is possible to get an overall picture while also being able to look at all the details. Using techniques for *analysis*, it is possible to identify potential drawbacks such as bottlenecks and fail points, and study solutions to overcome them. By using computer-understandable languages, it is possible to conduct simulations of interactions and behavior of service systems to aid managerial and operational decisions. Methods similar to process mining [22] can be used to obtain insights on how services are provisioned.

Multi-perspective.   A white-box service system modeling tool can generate different service description views based on the stakeholder accessing the model and its objective. In other words, service systems can have *multi-perspectives*. Hence, customers may obtain a service description such as the one provided by Linked USDL; staff can obtain a description view depicting internal operations; and so forth. Those are all different views of the same service system.

Automation. The use of computer-understandable languages also enables to increase the level of *automation* of tasks, e.g., the automated generation of service documentation for customers and staff to better understand services. Documentation facilitates staff training and customers knowledge about service offerings. It is also possible to read service models, schedule and dispatch workers, and assign resources to complete service provisioning.

These benefits can foster the development of theories, methods, and tools to enable organizations and societies to converge towards economies which are truly service-based and service-driven.

1.5 Definitions

Despite the importance of the service sector, there is still no accepted definitions for the various terms related to the concept of service [2]. Different meanings have generated inconsistencies not only across disciplines, but also within them [23]. Therefore, it is necessary to disambiguate the meaning of service terms and provide clarifications to be used as a shared understanding. We do not aim to create new definitions. We seek to provide brief summaries for common service related terms from existing definitions found in the literature.

According to the ITIL library, "a service is a means of delivering value to customers by facilitating outcomes customers want to achieve without the ownership of specific costs and risks" [24]. The W3C[5] defines service as "an abstract resource that represents capability of performing tasks that form a coherent functionality from the point of view of provider entities and requester entities. To be used, a service must be realized by a concrete provider agent" [25]. Hill states that "a service may be defined as a change in the condition of a person, or a good belonging to some economic unit, with the prior agreement of the former person or economic unit" [26]. Based on these definitions from various fields (e.g., IT management, computer science, and economics) and also from other authors (c.f. [2, 23, 27–29]), we can provide the following definition for the term service:

Definition 1.1 A *service* is a previously agreed exchange of competences and knowledge between a provider and a customer in order to provide value to both parties.

When studying services, we are faced with other terms that need clarification, namely *service system, service model, service instances, service description*, and *business model*.

A service system is described in the literature as "[...] a system comprised of facilitator and appraiser systems for generating value through the provision and consumption of services" [30], "[...] complex adaptive systems made up of people, [...] dynamic and open, rather than simple and optimized" [2], among other definitions (e.g., [27, 29, 31–33]). Therefore, we can provide the following definition:

---

[5] World Wide Web Consortium: http://www.w3.org.

Definition 1.2 A *service system* is a collection of resources, stakeholders, processes and other service assets that, combined, enable value co-creation between producer and consumer.

Models "[...] help by letting us work at a higher level of abstraction [...] by hiding or masking details, bringing out the big picture, or by focusing on different aspects" [34]. Their essence is abstraction: "[...] the removal of fickle and distracting detail of implementation technologies as well as the use of concepts that allow more direct expression of phenomena in the problem domain. [...] the only effective means that we have of dealing with complexity that overwhelms our cognitive capacities" [35]. Crossing these statements with others in the literature (e.g., [36, 37]), we reach the following definition for service model:

Definition 1.3 A *service model* is an abstraction of a service system that highlights its structure, its elements, and the relations between elements, hiding its complex nature from who does not need to know it.

Modeling is the activity of creating abstractions and representations, i.e., models, of a service system to provide guidelines for its design, implementation, deployment, and management. Each service model is created to answer important questions about the characteristics, behavior, and structure of a service: M is a model of a service S if M can be used to answer questions about the characteristics and structures of service S.

Each service model is an abstraction of a service system. It is created through abstraction by ignoring some aspects of a service to highlight other more important characteristics. An abstraction is a generalization of content and/or suppression of details to allow for a broader view, decrease complexity, or focus on a specific viewpoint. A common way to raise the level of abstraction is to rely on models, architectures, business rules, and metamodels. The best model, indeed, should be the result of a balance between realism and simplicity since it is an abstract representation of reality. As a rule, and in most modeling efforts, details that are unnecessary are not included.

While the model consists of classes, representing things of significance for a service system and relationship assertions about associations between pairs of classes, a service instance assigns actual values for those classes.

Definition 1.4 A *service instance* (or *service description*) is an instance of a model. It captures the information describing a particular service. It is the result or output of the activity of service modeling.

Service descriptions "[...] bring various ways to describe services' interfaces using schema, models and semantics" [38]. A service description is a descriptive representation of (part of) a service system used to educate the different stakeholders about its properties and interactions.

A business model is defined by Timmers [39] as "[...] an architecture for the product, service and information flows, including a description of the various business actors and their roles, a description of the potential benefits for the various business actors, and a description of the sources of revenue". Osterwalder and Pigneur [40] state that "a business model describes the rationale of how an organization creates, delivers, and captures value". Based on these descriptions and other definitions found in the literature (e.g., [41–44]), we can summarize the definition of business model as follows:

Definition 1.5 A *business model* is a conceptual representation of the business of an organization intended to describe its services, stakeholders, interactions, value propositions, explanations on how the organization meets customer goals, and how it makes profit.

Figure 1.3 builds on the terms explored previously to contextualize the scope of a service system model like the one we intend to develop. A business model is a higher-level model that contains many service systems. A service system is modeled by one or more service models, which may contain models for its internal elements, such as process models. Different stakeholders can "see" a service system from views perspectives by accessing various service descriptions.

1.6 Objectives

Since previous work mainly took a black-box approach, we now take the challenge of defining a model to describe a service system using a white-box approach. The model opens new doors for Service Science including service simulation and analytics and the automatic comparisons of different service systems. This is still a recent research field and, thus, not many contributions have been made so far. Most of them are conceptual.

This book approaches the development and implementation of a service system model by fulfilling four partial objectives:

1. **Conceptual Framework.** The first objective was to conduct an extensive research to identify the most common service model concepts found in the literature (c.f. [7, 40, 45–49]). A framework was developed to compare and contrast existing approaches. The most important concepts and building blocks were identified and a conceptual model to capture service systems was developed (see Sects. 3.2 and 3.3).
2. **Model Implementation.** The second objective was to implement the conceptual model (see Sect. 3.5). The implemented model, called Linked Service System for USDL (LSS-USDL), was build using Semantic Web technologies and its construction followed Linked Data principles [50]. The model was build with RDF[6], the standard for Linked Data, and reused existing vocabularies found in the Linked Data Cloud (to maximize compatibility and reusability and minimize

---

[6] Resource Description Framework.

engineering efforts) making use of the recent developments towards organizations and governments publishing data on the web [51].

3. **Service Programming.** A third objective was to demonstrate how a real-world service system could be modeled with LSS-USDL (see Sect. 4.2) and how it could be accessed and queried programmatically (see Sect. 4.3). The service system modeled was the Incident Management (IM) service from the Information Technology Infrastructure Library (ITIL), a set of best practices for IT service management widely adopted by large enterprises. The programming language used was Python since libraries to access and modify RDF models are available and are stable.

4. **Service Tooling.** For the model to be accepted by managers, and other non-technical service system modelers, tools need to be available. Hence, the fourth objective was to develop a tool that hides technical details and is easy to use and understand (see Sect. 5.1). This creates the challenge of hiding as much complexity as possible while still making full use of the capabilities of the model. It also requires a basic understanding about what is cognitively difficult for users and what metaphors may be used. Ideally, service description languages capturing different views should interoperate. Thus, Sect. 5.3 acts as a proof of concept to show that it is possible to export/import an LSS-USDL service model into/from the Linked USDL service description language. This type of interoperability demonstrates that a black-box and white-box perspectives can co-exist.

The white-box perspective on services given by LSS-USDL brings several benefits for organizations. The degree of automation of service delivery and provisioning can increase since service systems are fully modeled with a computer-understandable language.

References

1. Robert Glushko and Lindsay Tabas. Designing service systems by bridging the front stage and back stage. Information Systems and e-Business Management, 7:407–427, 2009.
2. Jim Spohrer, Paul Maglio, John Bailey, and Daniel Gruhl. Steps toward a science of service systems. Computer, 40(1):71–77, January 2007.
3. Holger Luczak, Christian Gill, and Bernhard Sander. Architecture for Service Engineering The Design and Development of Industrial Service Work. In Dieter Spath and Klaus-Peter Fähnrich, editors, Advances in Services Innovations, pages 47–63. Springer, Berlin Heidelberg, 2007.
4. Henry Chesbrough and Jim Spohrer. A research manifesto for services science. Communications of the ACM, 49(7):35–40, 2006.
5. Paul Maglio, Savitha Srinivasan, Jeffrey Kreulen, and Jim Spohrer. Service systems, service scientists, SSME, and innovation. Communications of the ACM, 49(7):81–85, 2006.
6. Stephen Vargo and Robert Lusch. Evolving to a new marketing dominant logic for marketing. Journal of Marketing, 68(1):1–17, 2004.
7. Andreas Zolnowski, Martin Semmann, and Tilo Böhmann. Introducing a Co-Creation Perspective to Service Business Models. In Enterprise Modelling and Information Systems Architectures (EMISA), page 243, 2011.
8. Thomas Erl. Service-Oriented Architecture: Concepts, Technology, and Design. Prentice Hall PTR, Upper Saddle River, NJ, USA, 2005.

9. Carlos Pedrinaci, John Domingue, and Amit Sheth. Handbook on Semantic Web Technologies, volume Semantic Web Applications, chapter Semantic Web Services. Springer, 2010.
10. OMG. Service oriented architecture Modeling Language (SoaML) Specification, 2012.
11. Matthew MacKenzie, Ken Laskey, Francis McCabe, Peter Brown, and Rebekah Metz. Reference Model for Service Oriented Architecture 1.0.
12. The Open Group. Service-Oriented Architecture Ontology, 2010.
13. John Domingue, Michal Zaremba, Barry Norton, Mick Kerrigan, Adrian Mocan, Alessio Carenini, Emilia Cimpian, Marc Haines, and James Scicluna. Reference Ontology for Semantic Service Oriented Architectures Version 1.0, 2008.
14. Mike Papazoglou. Web Services: Principles and Technology. Prentice Hall, 2012.
15. Hans Akkermans, Ziv Baida, Jaap Gordijn, Nieves Pena, Ander Altuna, and Inaki Laresgoiti. Value webs: Using ontologies to bundle real-world services. IEEE Intelligent Systems, 19(4):57–66, July 2004.
16. Martin Hepp. GoodRelations Language Reference, 2011.
17. Carlos Pedrinaci, Jorge Cardoso, and Torsten Leidig. Linked USDL: A Vocabulary for Webscale Service Trading. In 11th Extended Semantic Web Conference, Crete, Greece, May 2014.
18. Jorge Cardoso, Alistair Barros, Norman May, and Uwe Kylau. Towards a unified service description language for the internet of services: Requirements and first developments. In Services Computing (SCC), 2010 IEEE International Conference on, pages 602–609. IEEE, 2010.
19. Jorge Cardoso, Konrad Voigt, and Matthias Winkler. Service Engineering for The Internet of Services. In Enterprise Information Systems X, volume 19, pages 17–25. Springer, 2008.
20. Christian Bizer, Tom Heath, and Tim Berners-Lee. Linked Data - The Story So Far. International Journal on Semantic Web and Information Systems, 5(3):1–22, 2009.
21. Henry Chesbrough. Open innovation: The new imperative for creating and profiting from technology. Harvard Business Press, 2003.
22. Wil van der Aalst. Process Mining: Discovery, Conformance and Enhancement of Business Processes. Springer Publishing Company, Incorporated, 1st edition, 2011.
23. Roberta Ferrario, Nicola Guarino, Christian Janiesch, Tom Kiemes, Daniel Oberle, and Florian Probst. Towards an ontological foundation of services science: The general service model. Wirtschaftsinformatik, Switzerland, pages 16–18, 2011.
24. OGC. The Official Introduction to the ITIL Service Lifecycle. ITIL Series. Stationery Office, 2007.
25. W3C. Web services glossary, 2004.
26. Peter Hill. On Goods and Services. Review of Income and Wealth, 23(4):315–38, 1977.
27. Steven Alter. Service system fundamentals: Work system, value chain, and life cycle. IBM Systems Journal, 47(1):71–85, 2008.
28. Roberta Ferrario and Nicola Guarino. Towards an ontological foundation for services science. Future Internet-FIS 2008, pages 152–169, 2009.
29. Paul Maglio, Stephen Vargo, Nathan Caswell, and Jim Spohrer. The service system is the basic abstraction of service science. Information Systems and e-business Management, 7(4):395–406, 2009.
30. Manuel Mora, Rory O'Connor, Mahesh Raisinghani, Jorge Macías-Luévano, and Ovsei Gelman. An it service engineering and management framework (its-emf). International Journal of Service Science, Management, Engineering, and Technology (IJSSMET), 2(2):1–15, 2011.
31. Ketki Dhanesha, Alan Hartman, and Anshu Jain. A model for designing generic services. In Services Computing, 2009. SCC'09. IEEE International Conference on, pages 435–442. IEEE, 2009.
32. Manuel Mora, Mahesh Raisinghani, Ovsei Gelman, and Miguel-Angel Sicilia. Onto-servsys: A service system ontology. The Science of Service Systems, pages 151–173, 2011.
33. Robert Glushko. Seven contexts for service system design. Handbook of service science, pages 219–249, 2010.
34. OMG. Introduction to OMG's Unified Modeling Language (UML), 2012.
35. Bran Selic. UML 2.0: Exploiting Abstration and Automation, 2004.

36. Eva Söderström, Birger Andersson, Paul Johannesson, Erik Perjons, and Benkt Wangler. Towards a framework for comparing process modelling languages. In Advanced Information Systems Engineering, pages 600–611. Springer, 2006.
37. Jang-Eui Hong and Doo-Hwan Bae. Software modeling and analysis using a hierarchical object-oriented Petri net. Information Sciences, 130(1):133–164, 2000.
38. Jorge Cardoso, Carlos Pedrinaci, Torsten Leidig, Paulo Rupino, and Peter De Leenheer. Open semantic service networks. In International Symposium on Services Science (ISSS), Leipzig, Germany, 2012.
39. Paul Timmers. Business models for electronic markets. Electronic markets, 8(2):3–8, 1998.
40. Alexander Osterwalder and Yves Pigneur. Business model generation: a handbook for visionaries, game changers, and challengers. Wiley, 2010.
41. Mutaz Al-Debei. The design and engineering of innovative mobile data services: An ontological Framework founded on business model thinking. School of Information Systems, Computing and Mathematics, 2010.
42. Edward Faber, Pieter Ballon, Harry Bouwman, Timber Haaker, Oscar Rietkerk, and Marc Steen. Designing business models for mobile ict services. In Workshop on concepts, metrics & visualization, at the 16th Bled Electronic Commerce Conference eTransformation, Bled, Slovenia, 2003.
43. Joan Magretta. Why business models matter. Harvard business review, 80(5):86–93, 2002.
44. Alexander Osterwalder, Yves Pigneur, and Christopher Tucci. Clarifying business models: Origins, present, and future of the concept. Communications of the association for Information Systems, 16(1):1–25, 2005.
45. Rainer Alt and Hans-Dieter Zimmermann. Preface: introduction to special section-business models. Electronic Markets, 11(1):3–9, 2001.
46. Erwin Fielt. An Extended Business Model Canvas for Co-Creation and Partnering. http:// fieltnotes.blogspot.pt/2010/12/extended-business-model-canvas-for-co.html, 2010
47. Jim Spohrer and Paul Maglio. Service science: Toward a smarter planet. Introduction to service engineering, pages 3–30, 2009.
48. Reuven Karni and Maya Kaner. An engineering tool for the conceptual design of service systems. Advances in Services Innovations, pages 65–83, 2007.
49. Sybren Kinderen and Jaap Gordijn. Reasoning about substitute choices and preference ordering in e-services. In Advanced Information Systems Engineering, pages 390–404. Springer, 2008.
50. Tim Berners-Lee. Linked Data - Design Issues, 2006.
51. Sebastian Speiser and Andreas Harth. Towards linked data services. In Proceedings of the 9th International Semantic Web Conference (ISWC), 2010.

Chapter 2
Conceptual Frameworks

This chapter presents four theories from different academic disciplines that provide a comprehensive view of service. According to Gregor's taxonomy of theory types [1], the theories presented are theories for analysis. This means that they offer concepts to describe, understand and analyze an object of study (i.e., what is), but do not explain or predict phenomena (i.e., why something is or what will be), nor provide prescriptions to create objects or cause events (i.e., how to do something).

2.1 Major Theories

The four reviewed theories are suitable for developing a concept base that can be used for selecting concepts when designing a conceptual service system model as the basis for the LSS-USDL service description language (see Chap. 3). The service concepts described by these theories constitute an inter-disciplinary knowledge base that allows achieving rigor when designing the intended model and language, providing a theoretical foundation and justification for their construction [2].

The theories selected for this chapter are:

- Service-Dominant Logic [3] (Sect. 2.2).
- Unified Services Theory [4] (Sect. 2.3).
- Work system metamodel [5] (Sect. 2.4).
- Resource-Service-System model [6] (Sect. 2.5).

The Service-Dominant Logic is a descriptive theory of service from the Marketing discipline. It has been proposed as the philosophical basis of the new inter-disciplinary field of Service Science, Management, and Engineering (SSME)—Service Science in short—which studies service systems with the aim of creating the systemic knowledge required for sustainable service innovation [7].

To complement the marketing perspective of service, with its strong emphasis on the creation of customer benefits, the second reviewed theory is drawn from

© The Author(s) 2014
J. Cardoso et al., *Service Systems*,
SpringerBriefs in Computer Science, DOI 10.1007/978-3-319-10813-1_2

the Operations Management discipline. The Unified Services Theory describes the service production process and allows analyzing the efficiency and quality of this process. Thirdly, a "work system" perspective, i.e., viewing an object of study as a system in which work is performed, allows understanding service as a system (socio-technical or automated) in an organizational context [8]. The Work system metamodel provides an operational view of service systems (and work systems in general) that offers the basis for detailed analysis of the system's form, function and environment [9].

This operational view is finally complemented by an economic view that also considers aspects related to the exchange of service. This view is obtained through application of the Resource-Event-Agent ontology, originally from the Accounting discipline, as a model of economic exchange. Applying this ontology to service systems has resulted in the Resource-Service-System model of service exchange, which is the fourth theory presented in this chapter.

The combination of theories from multiple disciplines, each offering a partial perspective on service, leads to the creation of a more complete concept base that covers different economic, management, and engineering aspects related to service. This ambition is fully in line with the purpose of the new SSME field as it is with the design of a conceptual model of service system that can serve as the foundation of a white-box service description language.

The next sections will present the selected descriptive theories of service. To build the concept base for the intended service system conceptualization, an integrated concept map with concepts from the different theories is gradually constructed throughout Sects. 2.2–2.5. A summary is given in Sect. 2.6.

2.2 Service-Dominant Logic

The growing importance of service and service systems and the rising demand for service innovation and, hence, increasing investments in service R&D have often been motivated by the global sectorial shift in gross domestic product and employment from agriculture and industry to service (see, e.g., [10]). The difference between the declining second economic sector and the rising third sector is traditionally (and officially in governmental reports) made on the basis of the output of economic actors, producing either goods (second sector) or services (third sector).

Services are seen as products that are different from goods in terms of the IHIP characteristics: intangibility, heterogeneity, inseparability (of production and consumption), and perishability [11]. From a management perspective, the IHIP characteristics are considered as shortcomings, making it more difficult to properly handle services, e.g., with respect to their design, production, quality assurance, and marketing. To find answers to these shortcomings, dedicated service research disciplines like service management, service operations, service design, service engineering, etc. emerged.

2.2.1 A New Service Definition

The IHIP characteristics as distinguishing features between goods and services are not without their own shortcomings, casting doubts on the usefulness of separate service research disciplines like service marketing [12]. The Service-Dominant Logic [3, 13, 14] is the outcome of a counter-movement to the separate treatment (and researching) of the service sector. It promotes an economic world view in which all economic exchange is seen as the exchange of service for service.

According to Service-Dominant Logic, *service* is the application of one's competences for the benefit of someone else. Both goods and services (according to the traditional economic classification) can be used in the act of applying competences for the benefit of someone else. Hence, whether something officially classifies as a good or service is of minor importance as it is the act of applying competences that matters. The actual benefits of this act (i.e., service in singular) are determined by the beneficiary in terms of value-in-use (i.e., what utility is assigned to the application of competences) and value-in-context (i.e., how are the benefits experienced in the subjective ad-hoc context of the beneficiary), rather than value-in-exchange (i.e., what is the monetary value of the goods or services (in plural) when exchanging them).

2.2.2 Foundational Premises

The descriptive theory of Service-Dominant Logic has been expressed through the following set of ten foundational premises (FPs) [15]:

FP 1.   Service is the fundamental basis of exchange.
FP 2.   Indirect exchange masks the fundamental basis of exchange.
FP 3.   Goods are a distribution mechanism for service provision.
FP 4.   Operant resources are the fundamental source of competitive advantage.
FP 5.   All economies are service economies.
FP 6.   The customer is always a co-creator of value.
FP 7.   The enterprise cannot deliver value, but only offer value propositions.
FP 8.   A service-centered view is inherently customer oriented and relational.
FP 9.   All social and economic actors are resource integrators.
*FP*10.   Value is always uniquely and phenomenologically determined by the beneficiary.

The first foundational premise (FP1) recognizes that what economic actors exchange is the application of each other's competences. This fundamental axiom of Service-Dominant Logic goes back to 18th century economist Adam Smith's views on efficiency in economic activity through specialization [16].

Economic actors specialize in what they are best at doing based on their own knowledge and skills. Economic exchange occurs when actors apply their own specialized competences for the benefit of others. In this sense all economies are service economies (FP5) rendering the official classification in economic sectors irrelevant.

For instance, farmers (first sector) specialize in crop growing and apply their competences in doing so to feed animals and people. But rather than having farmers work our own gardens, they sell us their crop in which they have invested their crop growing skills and knowledge, hence, goods are a distribution mechanism for service provision (FP3).

Likewise, manufacturers (second sector) specialize in goods production and apply their competences in doing so to satisfy people's needs for goods for which they lack the competences to produce themselves. But of course, to make the actual exchange of "I do this for you when you do this for me" efficient, money was invented; hence, indirect exchange (e.g., goods for money) masks the fundamental basis of exchange (FP2). As a final example, a service company or professional like a hairdresser (third sector) specializes in service provision and applies its or his competences in doing so to satisfy people's needs for services for which they lack the competences to provide for themselves. In case of the hairdresser, the essence of these specialized competences are not the goods like scissors, shampoo, hair gel, etc. which are only used as appliances through which the specialized hairdressing competences are conveyed, and which can easily be acquired by the customers themselves. The essence is the knowledge and skills related to hairdressing, which is far more difficult to acquire (and apply to oneself). Hence, FP4 states that *operant resources*, meaning skills and knowledge, are the fundamental source of competitive advantage.

The sixth foundational premise (FP6) introduces another fundamental concept of Service-Dominant Logic: *value co-creation*. Co-creation of value implies that the service beneficiary is always involved in the creation of value as he is the sole determiner of value (meaning value-in-use and value-in-context) (FP10) and the actor that applies specialized competences (i.e., operant resources) can only offer value propositions (FP7) which help to create value with and for the beneficiary. While the interactional nature of service is further stressed by FP8, the ninth foundational premise (FP9) introduces another activity of actors besides applying their specialized competences: *resource integration*. Actors need to integrate the resources they acquire as service beneficiaries into their own resources in order to survive and prosper, and to continue being able to apply specialized competences themselves. FP9 thus explains the exchange component in FP1.

2.2.3 Service-Dominant Logic Concepts

The concept map of Fig. 2.1 summarizes the key concepts that Service-Dominant Logic uses to describe service. *Resources* are of two kinds as determined by the service context under consideration: *operant resources* represent competences (i.e., knowledge and skills) or their embodiments (e.g., persons, organizational units, software agents, automated devices) that act upon other resources; *Operand resources* are resources that are acted upon or with like passive resources such as tools, materials, and data, but possibly also resources that may be active in another service context like persons, machines, and software. *Actors* exchange services by providing

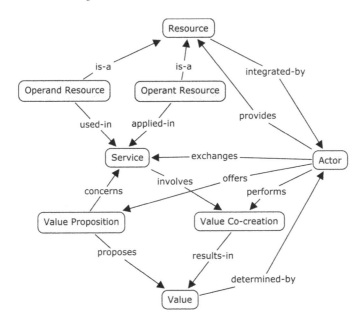

Fig. 2.1 Concept map Service-Dominant Logic

resources. The acting of operant resources on operand resources is what is called *service*, meaning an actor applying competences for the benefit of another actor. Through the exchange of service for service actors integrate resources that are made available, accessible or more valuable (as determined by the service beneficiary) by other actors, into their own resources. *Value* is always co-created by the beneficiary actor. It is the beneficiary actor who determines whether a service resulted in *value*. Therefore, an actor can only offer a *value proposition* concerning some service and cannot solely create value for the beneficiary actor.

2.3 Unified Services Theory

The Unified Services Theory [4] was developed for providing a distinctive, yet integrative paradigm and common language for service management researchers. It is meant as a descriptive theory that defines concepts relevant to service management from a primarily, though not exclusive production perspective. As opposed to the Service-Dominant Logic, the Unified Services Theory recognizes the distinction between services and non-services. Its operational implications, therefore, address the challenges that are unique to the management of service processes.

2.3.1 Defining the Service Process

The theory does not define the concept of service directly, but talks about service processes. The object of study is the *production process*. An enterprise is a production system consisting of possibly multiple production processes.

The basic tenet of the Unified Services Theory is that a *service process* is a production process in which each individual consumer provides significant inputs. *Inputs* are resources available to production. Consumer inputs can be of three kinds: the consumer himself (e.g., going to a hairdresser), information provided by the consumer (e.g., providing information to a solicitor for preparing a legal case) or tangible belongings of the consumer (e.g., getting one's car repaired). Inputs that are not considered significant and hence do not allow qualifying a production process as a service process are general consumer feedback (e.g., a market research that provides ideas and requirements for a new product and, thus, informs production processes) and selecting and consuming the output from production processes. The latter activity is part of a *consumption process* in which consumers extract value by interacting with the output of production processes or with the service providers themselves.

The operational implications of the theory for service management focus strongly on what makes a production process a service process, i.e., the necessity of consumer inputs. For instance, according to the theory service quality depends in large part on the quality of the inputs that the consumer provides. Also, service processes can be made more efficient by reducing the variability in consumer inputs. Overall, it is the presence of consumer inputs that makes service processes harder to manage than non-service processes. The consumer-producer interaction required for service processes implies that consumers are also suppliers and, hence, service supply chains are always bidirectional [17].

2.3.2 Unified Services Theory Concepts

The main concepts of the Unified Services Theory are shown in Fig. 2.2. A process is a series of actions. Amongst different kinds of processes are production and consumption processes. Note that the theory also defines other kinds of processes like business processes and IT processes [18], but these are at this moment not relevant for understanding service. A production process is a process that transforms inputs into outputs. An *input* is a resource available to production. Generally, the *producers* that own the production processes provide inputs to these processes. *Service processes* are production processes in which also *consumers* provide or make available input resources (either themselves or information they have or their property). An *output* is a result of production. Consumers select outputs from production processes to satisfy their *needs*. The extraction of *value*, which is the satisfaction of consumers' needs, is performed in *consumption processes*. A concept not explicitly shown but present in the chain of relations in the concept map is that of consumer-producer

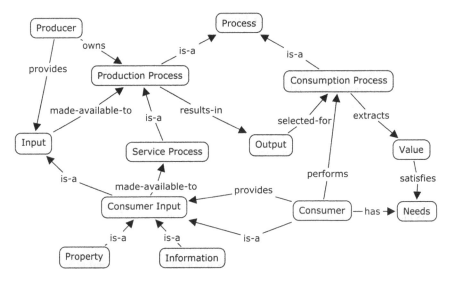

Fig. 2.2   Concept map Unified Services Theory

interaction, which is bidirectional. Consumers influence producers by providing production inputs and producers influence consumers by acting on the consumer inputs.

2.3.3   Service Process Versus Service as Process

Joining the concept maps of the Service-Dominant Logic and the Unified Services Theory is not an easy operation, given their fundamentally different view of service. While service is defined as a process in the Service-Dominant Logic, it is not the same as the service process as intended by the Unified Services Theory which employs a more restricted meaning and distinguishes between service and non-service situations (such distinction would be nonsense in Service-Dominant Logic). While service in the Service-Dominant Logic requires co-creation between the producer/provider and consumer/beneficiary, the acts of the service provider (or producer) and beneficiary (or consumer) might overlap completely or partially but also be completely independent in space and time; hence, the resource integration and resulting value capture by the beneficiary might happen long after and in a different location than the provider's activities. This scenario is consistent with what happens in the consumption process of the Unified Services Theory where the consumer may extract value from outputs of non-service production processes without any interaction with the producer. However, to qualify as a service process, the production process needs consumer inputs, which implies some degree of overlap in time and space between producer and consumer activities. As noted in [4], this interaction is, however, not as restrictive as requiring co-production as the provision of the consumer's labor is only one possible type of consumer input into the production process.

2.3.4 From Service Process to Service Exchange

The notion of value as satisfying needs in the Unified Services Theory is close to the notion of value-in-use in the Service-Dominant Logic, hence, value seems a common concept in both maps. Also in both theories it is the consumer/beneficiary that determines and captures the value. The resource integration in the Service-Dominant Logic and the value extraction to satisfy needs in the Unified Services Theory are, therefore, similar. To integrate both concept maps, value can, therefore, be used an anchor point. Further we see that consumer and producer in the Unified Services Theory are specializations (and actually roles) of actor in the Service-Dominant Logic. The inputs in the Unified Services Theory are resources in the Service-Dominant Logic.

As the purpose of the conceptual model we develop in this chapter is the creation of a concept base for the design of a white-box service description language and the Unified Services Theory offers more details on the "internals" of service, we start the integration from the concept map of this theory. Given the differences between both theories, the integrated concept map should allow for multiple interpretations of concepts to co-exist. Hence, we include in the concept map of Fig. 2.3 concepts

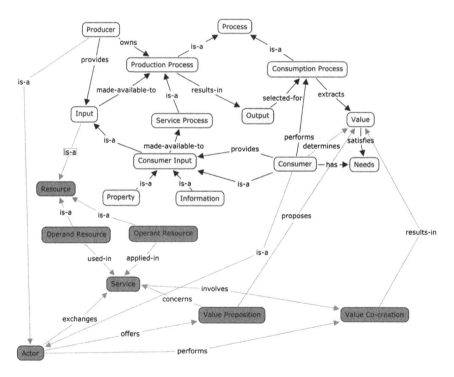

Fig. 2.3 Integrated concept map of the Unified Services Theory and the Service-Dominant Logic

from the Service-Dominant Logic to extend the concept map for the Unified Services Theory (Fig. 2.2), without claiming to have integrated the theories themselves.

Additions from the Service-Dominant Logic are the concepts of service, value co-creation and value proposition (though the latter concept is a component of the Unified Services Theory concept of business process, not shown here). Also, the distinction between operant and operand resources is added, e.g., a consumer providing his labor to the service process (i.e., co-production) would allow qualifying the consumer as an operant resource that is applied in the service (process). Also service exchange is a new element not covered by the Unified Services Theory. A further elaboration of the exchange nature of service is given in Sect. 2.5, where we introduce the Resource-Service-System model. In general we can see that the extension with concepts from the Service-Dominant Logic allows widening the Unified Services Theory's scope of service processes to service exchanges.

2.4 Work System Metamodel

The Work system metamodel [5] is an extension of the Work System Theory [19]. The Work System Theory defines a work system as a "system in which human participants and/or machines perform work (processes and activities) using information, technology, and other resources to produce specific products/services for specific internal and/or external customers" [19, p. 75]. Services are defined as acts performed to produce outcomes for the benefit of others. The Work System Theory encompasses a descriptive framework called Work System Framework that can be used to describe and analyze work systems. Given that service systems are work systems and most work systems are service systems (except those work systems not directed at others), the Work System Framework can be used to describe service systems. While the Work System Framework is intended to provide summary-level descriptions of work systems, the Work system metamodel expresses a more detailed operational view on work systems. In the remainder we will not use all these details (e.g., different types of technological, informational, and other resources used in service systems), but focus our discussion on concepts that might provide for interesting new additions to our current concept base (as in Fig. 2.3).

2.4.1 Work System Metamodel Concepts

The main concepts of interest of the Work system metamodel are shown in Fig. 2.4. A *service system* is a work system in which work is performed for the benefit of internal or external customers to the enterprise that offers the service. The benefits for an internal customer are other than for performing work activities within the service system itself. The service system contains *service system activities* that use *resources* and produce *products/services*. Resources can be *technological enti-*

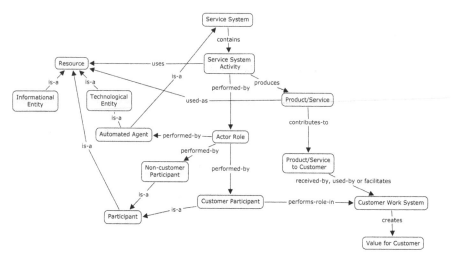

Fig. 2.4 Concept map Work system metamodel (simplified)

ties, informational entities, (human) *participants* or other resources. The term product/service refers to a bundle of tangible and/or intangible acts and outcomes that may be more goods-like or more services-like. Note that Work System Theory recognizes the traditional distinction between goods and services but does not consider it important to understand service systems. Service system activities are performed by *actor roles* which can be performed by *automated agents* (which is a technological entity and a totally automated service system on its own right), *non-customer participants* (e.g., an employee of the enterprise) or *customer participants* (i.e., in case of co-production). Products/services may be used as resources for other activities within the same service system, however, at least one product/service produced by an activity of the service system contributes to a *product/service to the customer*, meaning physical things, information, acts and/or outcomes used or received by a *customer work system* in which they facilitate the creation of *value for the customer*.

2.4.2 From Service Process to Service System

Comparing the Work system metamodel with the Unified Services theory, we see that the distinction between provider service system and customer work system is similar to that of production process and consumption process in the Unified Services Theory. Though not shown in Fig. 2.4, the Work system metamodel includes the concept of (business) process when two or more service system activities "are sufficiently interrelated and sequential enough to be considered a process" [5]. Hence, the production and consumption process are part of the provider, respectively customer work systems and contain themselves work system activities. A work system perspective, thus, allows describing Unified Services Theory processes in more detail, for instance by showing that the outputs of production process activities might be used as inputs for other activities within the same or different production process (belonging to the same provider work system), and, thus, not all outputs are directed at internal or external customers. Likewise, it can also show the resources of different kinds that are used as inputs in individual production process activities, whereas the Unified Services Theory focuses on different kinds of consumer inputs into the overall service process.

2.4.3 Reconciling Value Co-creation Definitions

The Work system metamodel is also interesting as it can help bridging the Unified Services Theory and the Service-Dominant Logic. The service brought about by the provider service system does not directly create value for the customer, but "facilitates" value creation [20], which is done in the customer work system. The product/service for customer is, thus, similar to the output of production processes that is selected for consumption processes in which value is extracted to satisfy consumer needs. Although the customer always has certain responsibilities, customer participation in service system activities (in the sense of co-production) is optional, so the absence of a distinction between service systems (or service production processes as in the Unified Services Theory) and "non-service" systems (or non-service production processes as in the Unified Services Theory) is similar to the Service-Dominant Logic where all economic activity is service (i.e., Foundational Premise FP5). Also, the definition of service is very similar to that of the Service Dominant Logic.

An apparent difference with the Service-Dominant Logic is the view of value co-creation which is optional in the Work system metamodel but strictly required for service in the Service-Dominant Logic. The difference is actually more a difference in definition as the value creation in the customer work system based on the products/services of the provider service system is what resource integrators (FP9) do and what qualifies as value co-creation in the Service-Dominant Logic. The Work system metamodel employs a more restrictive notion of value co-creation as customer work system activities that coincide in time and location with provider service system activities, implying that value co-creation is a more narrow form of co-production. More important is that the service system produces a "service as a process" (as in the Service-Dominant Logic), which facilitates value creation by customers/consumers (as in the Unified Services Theory).

The concept map in Fig. 2.5 shows how the Work system metamodel can be linked to both the Unified Services Theory and the Service-Dominant Logic. The product/service for customer is equated with the output that the consumer selects for the consumption process in the Unified Services Theory. Hence, the value for customer created by the customer work system is the value that is extracted in the consumption process performed by the consumer. The link with the Service-Dominant Logic is that service is performed by the service system.

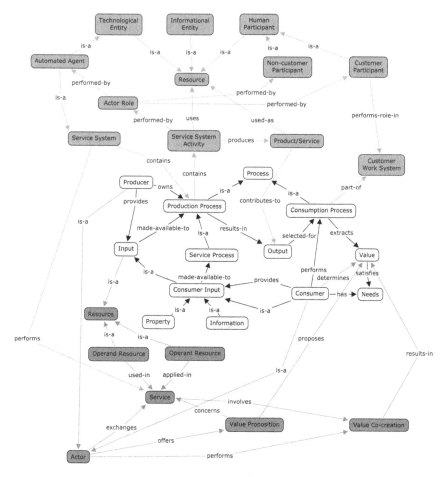

Fig. 2.5 Integrated concept map of the Unified Services Theory, Service-Dominant Logic and Work system metamodel

2.5 Resource-Service-System Model

The Resource-Service-System model [6, 21] interprets the Resource-Event-Agent (REA) model of economic exchange [22] according to the Service-Dominant Logic. In REA, economic exchange results from the economic reciprocal actions (called economic events) of independent entities (called economic agents) that provide each other the resources that they control (called economic resources).

2.5.1 Resource-Service-System Model Concepts

Rooted in Accounting, REA employs the traditional economic classification of products as goods and services, hence, services are a type of resource exchanged between economic agents. This means that a service resource (e.g., a consulting service) and the event that transfers this resource from a providing agent to a receiving agent (e.g., the contracting and executing of the consulting service) are explicitly distinguished, whereas such distinction is not recognized in the Service-Dominant Logic (i.e., the consulting process is the service).

The Resource-Service-System model, therefore, replaces the REA notion of economic resource by the Service-Dominant Logic notion of *operant/operand resource* (see the concept map in Fig. 2.6), the REA notion of economic event by the Service-Dominant Logic notion of *service* (as operant resources acting upon operand resources (e.g., as service target) or with operand resources (e.g., as tools or appliances)), and the REA notion of economic agent by that of *service system entity*. The latter concept is inspired by systems thinking in Service Science [23], where service systems are seen as supra-systems composed of sub-systems (i.e., service system entities) that improve their state (and, hence, the state of the supra-system) through service exchange.

As dynamic configurations of resources, service system entities possess the means to engage in *service exchanges* with other service system entities. Based on the REA axiom of economic reciprocity in economic exchange, also described as the duality of economic events, the Resource-Service-System model posits that service exchange is the reification of the dual relationship between economic reciprocal events as a series of actions and interactions undertaken by service system entities. Figure 2.6

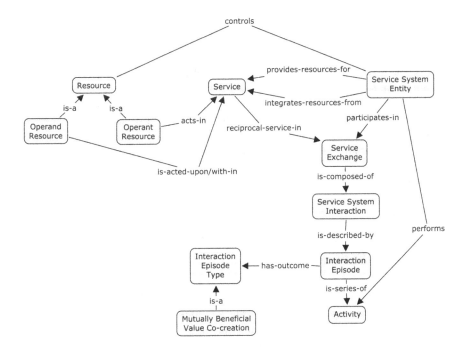

Fig. 2.6 Concept map Resource-Service-System model

shows that a service exchange is composed of *service system interactions* which are described by an *interaction episode* [24]. Such an interaction episode represents a series of activities, separately or jointly performed by the service system entities, as they occur in reality and, thus, lead to a certain outcome or interaction episode type. The purpose of service exchange is *mutually beneficial value co-creation*, meaning that service system entities engaging in service exchange employ their resources to integrate them with the exchange partner's resources in order to jointly create value for all parties. Whereas mutually beneficial value co-creation is the intended favorable outcome of service exchange, the model recognizes other possible (and unfavorable) outcomes in line with the ISPAR model of service interaction outcomes [24].

2.5.2 Mutually Beneficial Value Co-Creation

The Resource-Service-System model fully adheres to the service-dominant economic world view put forward by the Service-Dominant Logic. Therefore, both descriptive theories are very similar and concepts like operant/operand resource and service are shared. Further, while the Service-Dominant Logic does not employ the term service system, it is clear that the actor concept is the same as the service system entity concept in the Resource-Service-System model. The integrated concept map of Fig. 2.7, therefore, replaces the actor concept by the service system entity concept. Nevertheless, adding the Resource-Service-System model further enriches the conceptual model of service that we gradually built throughout this section. First, the Resource-Service-System model stresses more than the Service-Dominant Logic does that in an economic context, service is exchanged for service through interactions between service system entities. The kernel concept of the model is service exchange, not service. As a corollary, while the Service-Dominant Logic focuses on value co-creation as the creation of value by two actors for one of them, the Resource-Service-System model clarifies that the purpose of service exchange is mutually beneficial value co-creation, i.e., value is created jointly for both service beneficiaries. Second, the Resource-Service-System model recognizes (like the work system perspective described in [5] does) that this intended outcome might differ from the actual outcome of the interactions between service system entities.

2.5.3 From Service System to Service Exchange Between Service System Entities

The detailing of service exchange in terms of interactions between service system entities, in the form of joint and/or separate activities, provides for bridges with the two theories that focus more on the production/operational side of service processes and systems. Clearly, a service system activity as in the Work system metamodel is

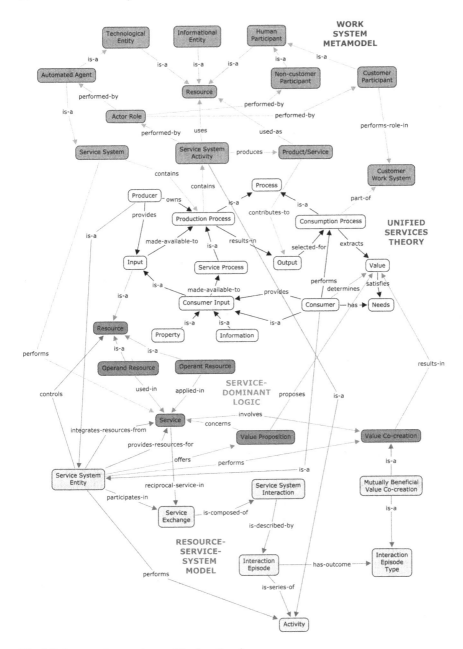

Fig. 2.7 Integrated concept map of the four theories

an activity as defined by the Resource-Service-System model, however, this is also true for an activity in the customer work system (coinciding or not with a provide service system activity). The concept of interaction episode is defined similarly to the concept of process in the Unified Services Theory, though it is used to represent the actual conduct of the activities in a single instance of service execution and should, therefore, be distinguished from a process "model". The service system concept of the Work system metamodel is different from the service system entity in the Resource-Service-System model as a service system entity (or actor in the Service-Dominant Logic; hence, producer/consumer in the Unified Services Theory) needs a work system (containing production processes) to perform a service.

A service system entity can itself be a resource in a "larger" work system. This is consistent with the systemic view of the Resource-Service-System model (i.e., a service system entity can be used as an operant resource that acts in a service that is exchanged by the supra-entity controlling the entity), but also covers scenarios like consumers that are used as input in service processes according to the Unified Services Theory and fully automated service systems that perform actor roles in activities of a higher-level service system as made possibly by the Work system metamodel. The operational details of the Work system metamodel surpass that of the Resource-Service-System model, but on the other hand service exchange as a concept is missing, which makes the integration valuable as it allows creating a more complete concept base for identifying the elements that compose a service system conceptualization for designing the intended white-box service description language.

2.6 Summary and Conclusions

At the end of this chapter we wish to stress that the concept map shown in Fig. 2.7 was obtained by gradually integrating the concept maps of the selected theories. Where possible, concepts from different theories with identical or very similar definitions were united. This way also relationships that cross theoretical boundaries could be established. The map shown in Fig. 2.7 is, however, not a conceptual model of an integrated descriptive theory of service due to some fundamental differences in view on the nature of service and value creation. Therefore, multiple interpretations of service and value creation co-exist.

All four theories consider service as an "occurrent" or "perdurant" rather than a "continuant" or "endurant", meaning *something that happens* rather than *something that exists*. While the definition of service in the Service-Dominant Logic, the Work system metamodel, and the Resource-Service-System model is (almost) identical, i.e., service is defined as a process in which something is done that benefits someone else, the Unified Services Theory, which does not directly define the concept of service, recognizes the existence of non-service processes. But as those non-service processes still produce outputs that consumers turn into benefits, the other three theories would argue that service was brought about.

The real difference in view on service depends on how service is "produced". The Unified Services Theory is clearly the most restrictive as service processes need individual consumer inputs, which, given the many kinds in which those inputs can exist, is still much broader than requiring services to be co-produced. Co-production is recognized by the Work system metamodel as customers participating as actors in the provider's service system activities, however, it is optional. There can be service without co-production, even without individual customer inputs that are made available to the provider's service system.

All four theories agree that the determination of value is the consumer/customer's business. For the Service-Dominant Logic and the Resource-Service-System model, this value capture by the service beneficiary is co-creation of value. For the Work system metamodel, this value capture, by the customer work system (or as in the Unified Services Theory, consumer's consumption process) is not co-creation unless activities in the customer work system coincide with activities in the provider service system. So there is a fundamental difference in the definition of value co-creation between on the one hand the Work system metamodel and on the other hand the Service-Dominant Logic and the Resource-Service-System model. Despite this different conceptualization of value co-creation, the notion of service is almost the same in these three theories.

The Resource-Service-System model adheres to the same service-dominant economic worldview as promoted by the Service-Dominant Logic and, hence, does not differ from that theory. It does stress, more than the Service-Dominant Logic does, the praxeology of service. Economic actors exchange service for their mutual benefit, hence, the exchange of service for service is a mutually beneficial value co-creation phenomenon. Further, it also recognizes, like the Work system metamodel does, that service is an outcome which is not always achieved, even when intended.

Despite these differences, we believe that the end result of our analysis and modeling exercise (Fig. 2.7), is a rich, multi-perspective concept base for designing a service system model that provides a conceptual foundation for the LSS-USDL language. Each of the reviewed theories has the ability to add concepts that are potentially relevant to a white-box service system conceptualization. The Service-Dominant Logic emphasizes that service is a process of operant resources acting upon operand resources. The Unified Services Theory sees the service production process as different from the value extraction process. The Work system metamodel adds operational details to service production, involving different kinds of operant and operand resources, and puts forward the notion of service system. Finally, the Resource-Service-System model adds the service exchange aspect and stresses that, in an economic context, value co-creation should be mutually beneficial. From a white-box perspective, this mutually beneficial value co-creation results from a series of activities, separately or jointly performed by service system entities, where these activities are part of the provider service system and/or customer work system, and can be organized as processes. Processes, activities, and resources used as inputs or produced as outputs, are all relevant concepts for a white-box service system conceptualization.

References

1. Shirley Gregor. The nature of theory in information systems. *MIS Q.*, 30(3):611–642, September 2006.
2. Alan Hevner, Salvatore March, Jinsoo Park, and Sudha Ram. Design science in information systems research. *MIS Q.*, 28(1):75–105, March 2004.
3. Stephen Vargo and Robert Lusch. Evolving to a new marketing dominant logic for marketing. *Journal of Marketing*, 68(1):1–17, 2004.
4. Scott Sampson and Craig Froehle. Foundations and implications of a proposed unified services theory. *Production and Operations Management*, 15(2):329–343, 2006.
5. Steven Alter. Work system perspective on service, service systems, it services, and service science. *Business Analytics and Information Systems*, 2014.
6. Geert Poels. The resource-service-system model for service science. In Juan Trujillo, Gillian Dobbie, Hannu Kangassalo, Sven Hartmann, Markus Kirchberg, Matti Rossi, Iris Reinhartz-Berger, Esteban Zimnyi, and Flavius Frasincar, editors, *Advances in Conceptual Modeling Applications and Challenges*, volume 6413 of *Lecture Notes in Computer Science*, pages 117–126. Springer, 2010.
7. Jim Spohrer, Paul Maglio, John Bailey, and Daniel Gruhl. Steps toward a science of service systems. *Computer*, 40(1):71–77, January 2007.
8. Steven Alter. Viewing services as service systems: basic premises of an operational model for service innovation, engineering, and management.*Working Paper*, 2014.
9. Steven Alter. Disentangling service: Using a work system perspective to reconcile different but overlapping portrayals of service and service systems. *Working Paper*, 2014.
10. IfM and IBM. *Succeeding through Service Innovation: A Service Perspective for Education, Research, Business and Government.* University of Cambridge Institute for Manufacturing, Cambridge, United Kingdom, 2008.
11. Arun Parasuraman, Valarie Zeithaml, and Leonard Berry. A Conceptual Model of Service Quality and Its Implications for Future Research. *The Journal of Marketing*, 49(4):41–50, 1985.
12. Stephen Vargo and Robert Lusch. The four service marketing myths: Remnants of a goods-based, manufacturing model. *Journal of Service Research*, 6(4):324–335, 2004.
13. Robert Lusch and Stephen Vargo. Service-dominant logic: reactions, reflections and refinements. *Marketing Theory*, 6:281–288, 2006.
14. Stephen Vargo and Robert Lusch. From goods to service(s): Divergences and convergences of logics. *Industrial Marketing Management*, 37(3):254–259, May 2008.
15. Stephen Vargo and Robert Lusch. Service-dominant logic: continuing the evolution. *Journal of the Academy of Marketing Science*, 36(1):1–10, 2008.
16. Stephen Vargo, Paul Maglio, and Melissa Akaka. On value and value co-creation: A service systems and service logic perspective. *European Management Journal*, 26(3):145–152, 2008.
17. Scott Sampson. Customer-supplier duality and bidirectional supply chains in service organizations. *International Journal of Service Industry Management*, 11:348–364, 2000.
18. Scott Sampson. A unified services theory paradigm for service science, June 2007.
19. Steven Alter. Work system theory: Overview of core concepts, extensions, and challenges for the future. *Journal of the Association for Information Systems*, 14(2), 2013.
20. Christian Grönroos. Value co-creation in service logic: a critical analysis. *Marketing Theory*, pages 279–301, 2011.
21. Geert Poels. A conceptual model of service exchange in service-dominant logic. In Jean-Henry Morin, Jolita Ralyté, and Mehdi Snene, editors, *Exploring Services Science*, volume 53 of *Lecture Notes in Business Information Processing*, pages 224–238. Springer, 2010.
22. Guido Geerts and William McCarthy. An ontological analysis of the economic primitives of the extended rea enterprise information architecture. *International Journal of Accounting Information Systems*, 3(1):1–16, 2002.

23. Manuel Mora, Mahesh Raisinghani, Rory O'Connor, and Ovsei Gelman. Toward an integrated conceptualization of the service and service system concepts: A systems approach. *IJISSS*, 1(2):36–57, 2009.
24. Paul Maglio, Stephen Vargo, Nathan Caswell, and Jim Spohrer. The service system is the basic abstraction of service science.*Information Systems and e-business Management*, 7(4):395–406, 2009.

Chapter 3
The LSS-USDL Model

In Chap. 2, we studied four theories that provided a comprehensive view of service. This chapter starts by complementing the study made by looking into business model conceptualizations to create an evaluation framework that will help in identifying a set of concepts to be used for the creation of a service system model. Once the concepts are identified, they will be structured and organized into what we call a 6-point interaction star model. The model, called LSS-USDL, was implemented using semantic web technologies.

3.1 Service System Evaluation Framework

Related research has proposed several business model conceptualizations. We briefly present eight of these proposals that are relevant to our research as they define concepts that pertain to both external and internal views of service systems. We do not explain these conceptualizations in detail, but merely list concepts relevant to a service system model. It should be noted that these proposals are unrelated to the service theories reviewed in the previous section, hence, both types of related work will be used in the next section to derive the most common service system concepts.

3.1.1 Business Model Conceptualizations of Service Systems

Alt and Zimmermann [4] distinguished six generic elements as a comprehensive framework to develop *business models*: Mission, Structure, Processes, Revenues, Legal issues and Technology. Published in 2001, this is the earliest proposal in our study, but as we can see by analyzing Table 3.1 it already mentions most of the generic concepts that newer models used the most. This indicates that it had an impact in the field.

© The Author(s) 2014   35
J. Cardoso et al., *Service Systems*,
SpringerBriefs in Computer Science, DOI 10.1007/978-3-319-10813-1_3

Table 3.1 Service model evaluation framework

	Goals	Stakeholders	Processes	Inputs	Outputs	Resources	Measures	Legal	Financial
Vargo and Lusch [1]	■	■	□	■	■	■		■	■
Sampson and Froehle [2]	■	■	■	■	■	■			
Poels [28]	■	■	■	■	■	■	□		■
Alter [3]	■	■	■	■		■	■	■	
Alt and Zimmermann [4]	■	■	■			□		■	□
Petrovic et al. [5]	■		■	■	■	■			■
Kaner and Karni [6]	■	□	■		■	■	□	□	□
Kinderen and Gordijn [9, 10]	■	■	□	■	■				□
Spohrer and Maglio [11]	■	■	■	■		■	■	□	
Osterwalder and Pigneur [12]	□	■	■			■			■
Fielt [13]	□	■	■	■		■			■
Zolnowski et al. [16]	□	■	■			■			■

empty = no contribution; □ = moderate contribution; ■ = important contribution

Petrovic et al. [5] divided a *business model* into seven sub-models: Value model, Resource model, Production model, Customer relations model (it was further divided into Distribution model, Marketing model and Service model), Revenue model, Capital model, and Market model. The naming of this model's elements hints at a lower level description for each of them. However, the authors do not identify any further characteristics.

Kaner and Karni [6, 7] proposed CAIOPHYKE, a service model based on 9 major classes: Customers, Goals, Inputs, Outputs, Processes, Human enablers, Physical enablers, Information enablers, and Environment. Each of these major classes can be further described by main classes, which can then be further described by their respective minor classes. This model was developed based on a study with 150 student projects that covered around 100 service domains [8]. This is one of the most comprehensive models found in the literature. However, it features a high level of complexity without a proper formalization, which prevents from creating an abstraction to handle complexity.

In e³service [9, 10], Kinderen and Gordijn focused on satisfying consumer needs and displaying the various value offerings from different services for an easier comparison. Therefore, the elements of this model are different from other approaches. This model is a valuable contribution to the state of the art as it is represented by a machine-readable ontology, the level of formality we envision for our model. However, its scope is customer-oriented, while we seek a manager-oriented approach that provides a view on how a service system operates.

Spohrer and Maglio [11] defined a service as value-cocreation and list ten related foundational concepts: Ecology, Entities, Interactions, Outcomes, Value proposition based interactions, Governance mechanism based interactions, Stakeholders, Measures, Resources, Access rights and Questions [11]. Table 3.1 shows that it is one of the most complete models of our study.

Osterwalder and Pigneur [12] propose the Business Model Canvas, a high-level graphical tool for business modeling. The model uses the concepts Value proposition, Customer segments, Channels, Customer relationships, Key activities, Key resources, Key partners, Cost structure, and Revenue Streams. This model and its tool are very simple and easy to understand and enjoy some popularity.

Fielt [13] extended the Business Model Canvas by addressing its strongest limitations: the lack of partnering (c.f. [14]) and co-creation (c.f. [15]) concepts. This increased the complexity of the original model. However, Table 3.1 shows that this new model only contributes to one more element of the common concepts, so there is a risk that this increase in complexity might not be beneficial.

Zolnowski et al. [16] tried to tackle the issue of lack of elements of the original Business Model Canvas to describe co-creation. This proposed approach focuses on a redistribution of the elements and their connections, rather than changing them as seen in Fielt's approach. Hence, this model shares the same concepts as the original Business Model Canvas, but their organization changes ([16] p.158).

3.1.2 Evaluation Framework

Comparing the related work reviewed in the previous chapter and section, it is possible to identify common concepts for describing service systems and, thus, derive a *service evaluation framework* of the most frequent and relevant concepts. The most common concepts identified are the Goals, Stakeholders, Processes, Inputs, Outputs, Resources, Measures, Legal and Financial (Table 3.1).

Goals are one of the most used concepts in the studied models. There is no doubt that this is a critical element for a service model, not only because of its wide acceptance among the studied approaches, but also because it states the objectives of the service system and its value proposition to consumers.

Stakeholders are one of the most important concepts of a service, since it is conditioned by the people and organizations involved. This concept is used by almost all the studied approaches due to its importance. In most service models, there is an attribute for service customers. In the Business Model Canvas from Osterwalder [12] and the two studied improved approaches there is also an attribute for service partners [12, 13, 16]. Spohrer and Maglio [11] propose additional attributes which specialize stakeholders into authorities and competitors.

Processes are, along with Goals, a concept that all studied approaches share. This concept is of utmost importance when describing services from an internal organization, because corporations must have a strong knowledge of the processes needed for their services, to identify bottlenecks, and other issues.

Inputs are described in a small set of service models. Spohrer and Maglio [11] refer to them using the concept of Ecology. Fielt [13], when extending the Business Model Canvas, adds Partner activities and Customer activities, which act as an input for the service. Karni and Kaner's CAIOPHYKE model [7] features the major class Inputs.

Outputs are also described in a small set of service models. Spohrer and Maglio [11] refer to them using the concept of Outcomes. e^{3}service [10] features outputs in the classes Consequence, Benefit, and Value derivation. Karni and Kaner [7] feature the major class Outputs.

Resources are described in most service description models, being absent just in e^{3}service. Alt and Zimmermann's approach [4] is the only model that does a partial description of this concept, focusing only on technology.

Measures refer to how the company can know its services' performance receive feedback of their operations. Only a small number of models were found in the literature that addressed this concept, as shown in Table 3.1.

Legal is the concept for the legal aspects of a service or business. It has a surprisingly low presence in the literature. Exceptions are Alt and Zimmermann [4] who propose Legal issues as one of their six generic elements of a business model; Karni and Kaner [7] use the main class Legal factors in the major class Environment; and Spohrer and Maglio identify Governance mechanism based interactions and Access rights [11].

`Financial` is the concept for the financial aspects of a service. This concept is used in most of the studied approaches. Hence, it is also an important concept for developing a comprehensive service model and evaluation framework.

3.2 Concepts and Building Blocks

The central concept of the service system model we propose is the notion of co-creation (which we will later call an interaction point). This concept shifts our study of economic activity from a Goods-Dominant logic (GD) where value exchange is perceived through goods transactions to a Service-Dominant logic (SD) where value exchange is co-created by all parties of service interactions [17]. Therefore, we no longer see value exchange as a provider delivering value to a customer by selling a product, but rather as both provider and customer co-creating value to each other during service interactions. Since co-creation during service interactions is a core feature of service systems and the interactions flow is also a core feature in service blueprints [18], we can conclude that a service system should be represented by its flow of interactions and their contextual information, such as the co-created value. Hence, we focus on describing service interactions, their context, and their flow.

The central concept of co-creation is complemented with a classification according to the interrogative pronouns commonly used in journalism: *what, how, where, who, when*, and *why*. It allows different people to look at the same service system from distinct perspectives by providing a holistic view on a system. The use of these pronouns has shown to be comprehensive for event-centered reporting [19]. This indicates that they may also be relevant to describe the events that are an integral elements of a service system. This strategy has shown to work well with the Zachman's framework for enterprise architecture [20] and other approaches by different authors in the field of information systems [21–23]. This classification enhances readability and understandability, gives an intuitive meaning to abstract concepts and helps organizations to ask questions about their processes and process models [23]. It also helps identifying some characteristics of a service offer and can be used as a common framework for querying different services [22].

Finally, the notion of co-creation and the interrogative pronouns are enriched with the concepts identified using the service model evaluation framework in the previous section. The framework combines the knowledge gathered by different authors in order to provide a set of concepts commonly used for the description of a service. The concepts are `Goals`, `Stakeholders`, `Processes`, `Inputs`, `Outputs`, `Resources`, `Measures`, `Legal`, and `Financial`.

One of our initial objectives was to avoid over-engineering the model. Thus, we followed a design philosophy which embraces the KISS principle[1] and parsimony to keep the final model simple. Our previous experience while developing the third

---

[1] KISS is an acronym and design principle for "Keep it simple, stupid" and was introduced by the U.S. Navy in 1960.

version of USDL [24] showed us that a model which tries to capture all the details of a domain becomes expensive, large, and more complex than necessary which harms its adoption and understanding.

3.3 Model Structure

The central element of the model is an `Interaction`. By matching the framework of common concepts discussed in the previous section with the interrogative pronouns, we obtain the concept `Stakeholders` for the pronoun "who", the concept `Goals` for the pronoun "why", the concept `Resource` for the pronoun "what", and the concept `Process` for the pronoun "how". The interrogative pronouns "when" and "where" are easily matched with the spatial and temporal context, respectively, of a service interaction. Furthermore, for a service system analysis, we can study the stakeholders' participation based on the actual roles that take part of an interaction. In addition, the flow of different resources can also be matched with the concepts `Input` and `Output`. Hence, we can describe service interactions with the six interrogative pronouns by using the following concepts:

- Who: `Role` (stakeholder; human or computer actor)
- Why: `Goal` (a service interaction goal)
- What: `Resource` (may be physical, knowledge or financial)
- How: `Process` (the business process a service interaction belongs to)
- When: `Time` (expresses temporal dependencies)
- Where: `Location` (the locations where service interactions occur)

The resulting structure is called a 6-point interaction star model for describing service interactions, as shown in Fig. 3.1.

Moreover, inspired by the work on service blueprinting [25], we may also classify interactions based on their area of action. A blueprint is a method created by Shostack [18] for analyzing a service delivery process by using a flow chart-like presentation to distinguish several types of customer interactions [26]. Thus, an interaction can be classified as a customer interaction, an onstage interaction, a backstage interaction, or a support interaction.

Fig. 3.1 6-point interaction star model

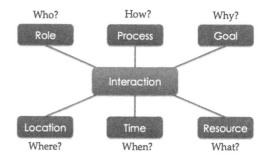

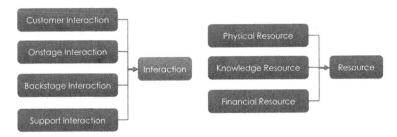

Fig. 3.2 Extensions to interaction and resource entities

The foundational ontology DOLCE (Descriptive Ontology for Linguistic and Cognitive Engineering) [27] classifies resources as endurants if they are physical objects or perdurants if they are not physical, such as services or events. Poels [28] classifies resources as operand if they are passive resources like objects or operant if they are knowledge and skills that embody competences. We can also find this pattern in some of the models we studied in the previous chapter. Therefore, resources should be classified as physical or knowledge. We also consider a third classification, financial resources, because of its importance for a business-oriented model.

Figure 3.2 shows these extensions to the interaction and resource entities. Naturally, more extensions can be added to the model, for example, for domain specific modeling (e.g., e-government, IT services, consulting services, or e-banking).

3.4 Implementation Technologies

The implementation of the model was called Linked Service System for USDL (LSS-USDL) and it was guided by two main objectives: (1) to use semantic web technologies to make the model computer-understandable and sharable, and (2) to enable the model to refer to data from the Linked Data Cloud (LDC) [29].

By bridging LSS-USDL and the LDC, service systems can be semantically enriched by establishing meaningful relationships with data present in the LDC, which includes information such as company names, locations, and traded resources stored in semantic data sources such as DBpedia (http://dbpedia.org), GeoNames (http://geonames.org), and WordNet (http://wordnet.princeton.edu).

3.4.1 The Semantic Web

The World Wide Web Consortium (W3C) started to work on the concept of a Semantic Web with the objective of developing solutions for data integration and interoperability. The goal was to develop ways to allow computers to interpret (sometimes termed understand) information in the web. The Semantic Web identifies a set of technologies and standards that form the basic building blocks of an infrastructure that supports the vision of the meaningful web.

LSS-USDL is a service system description schema that was formalized using two technologies from the Semantic Web: the Resource Description Framework (RDF) [30] and RDF Schema (RDFS) [31]. RDFS was used to define a schema and vocabulary to describe services. This schema is used to create RDF graphs that describe individual services. Both, RDF and RDFS, are used by applications that need to interpret and reason about the meaning of information instead of just parsing data for display purposes. This section will provide an overview of the main frameworks, languages, technologies, and knowledge bases behind the Semantic Web, namely, RDF, RDFS, Turtle notation, SPARQL, and Linked Data. Nonetheless, it does not aim to provide a comprehensive description of these technologies. Thus, the reader is also refereed to the book *Semantic Web for the Working Ontologist: Effective Modeling in RDFS and OWL* [32].

3.4.2 RDF

The resource description framework was developed by the W3C to provide a common way to describe information so it could be read and interpreted by computer applications. It was initially designed using XML (eXtensible Markup Language [33]) as the underlying syntax, which enables syntactic interoperability. RDF provides a graph model for describing resources on the web. A resource is an element (document, web page, printer, user, etc.) in the web that is uniquely identifiable by a universal resource identifier (URI). A URI serves as a means for identifying abstract or physical resources. For example, https://en.wikipedia.org/wiki/Incident_management identifies the location from where a web page about the ITIL Incident Management service can be obtained and the following encoding urn:isbn:1-420-09050-X identifies a book using its ISBN.

The RDF model is based on the idea of making statements about resources in the form of a subject-predicate-object expression, a triple in RDF terminology. Each element has the following meaning:

Subject is the resource; the "thing" that is being described.
Predicate is an aspect about a resource and expresses the relationship between the subject and the object.
Object is the value that is assigned to the predicate.

RDF is based on a very simple data model based on directed graphs. A set of nodes are connected by (directed) edges. Nodes and edges are labeled with identifiers (i.e., URI) that makes them distinguishable from each other and allows for the reconstruction of the original graph from the set of triples. RDF offers a limited set of syntactic constructs—only triples are allowed.

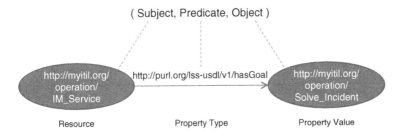

Fig. 3.3 An example of an RDF graph

Every RDF document is equivalent to an unordered set of triples, which describe a graph. For example, the RDF triple that describes the statement: "The goal of the ITIL Incident Management service is to solve incidents" is:

```
ı http://myitil.org/operation/IM_Service,
    http://w3id.org/lss-usdl/v1#hasGoal,
    http://myitil.org/operation/Solve_Incident
```

Listing 3.1 An RDF triple

The subject, `http://myitil.org/operation/IM_Service`, is a resource representing a particular ITIL service. This resource has the predicate (property) referenced by the URI `http://w3id.org/lss-usdl/v1#hasGoal` with the value `http://myitil.org/operation/Solve_Incident`. The statement can also be graphically represented as depicted in Fig. 3.3.

RDF blank nodes are used to express statements about individuals with certain properties without denominating the individual. The anonymity of blank nodes ensures that nothing besides the existence of the node can be inferred. Blank nodes, as the name suggests, may only occur in the subject or object position of a triple.

Literals describe data values. They may only occur as property values. Literals are represented as strings. A shared interpretation is assumed to be given. Therefore, literals can be typed with a data type, e.g., using the existing types from the XML Schema specification. Untyped literals are interpreted as strings.

3.4.3 Turtle Syntax

While RDF is a data model, there are several serialization formats that can represent RDF graphs. Originally, XML was proposed and has been widely adopted by RDF data processing and management tools. It is noteworthy that the data model is not affected by the choice of any of the serialization formats; the graph structures remain unchanged. Turtle, the Terse RDF Triple Language, is one of the serializations. It is a compact syntax for RDF that allows representing graphs in natural text form [34]. It will be used in the remainder of this chapter.

In Turtle, every triple is completed by a full stop. A URI is represented in angle brackets and literals are enclosed in quotation marks. White spaces outside identifiers and literals are ignored. One way to represent the RDF statement from Fig. 3.3 using Turtle is shown in Listing 3.2.

```
1   <http://myitil.org/operation/IM_Service>
        <http://w3id.org/lss-usdl/v1#hasGoal>
        <http://myitil.org/operation/Solve_Incident> .
```

Listing 3.2 Turtle syntax representation of the RDF graph in Fig. 3.3

Turtle allows for abbreviation that further increase the readability. For example, multiple triples with the same subject or triples with same subject and predicate can be pooled as shown in Listing 3.3.

```
1   @prefix rdf: <http://www.w3.org/1999/02/22-rdf-syntax-ns#> .
2   @prefix xsd: <http://www.w3.org/2001/XMLSchema#> .
3   @prefix geo: <http://www.w3.org/2003/01/geo/wgs84_pos#> .
4   @prefix myims: <http://myitil.org/operation#> .
5   @prefix lss-usdl: <http://w3id.org/lss-usdl/v1#> .
6
7   myims:IM_Service lss-usdl:hasGoal myims:Solve_Incident ;
8      rdf:type lss-usdl:ServiceSystem .
9
10  myims:Solve_Incident rdf:type lss-usdl:Goal .
11
12  myims:IMS12345 a myims:IM_Service ;
13     lss-usdl:Location [
14        geo:lat "48.7932" ;
15        geo:long "9.2258"
16     ] .
```

Listing 3.3 Turtle syntax representation of an RDF graph using abbreviations

The first lines introduce prefix abbreviations of the namespaces used. rdf:type (line 8) is a property to state that the resource myims:IM_Service is an instance of the class myims:Service system. The property rdf:type is often abbreviated to a. Capital first letters are used to indicate class names in contrast to individual and property names. The description of the location of the service myims:IMS12345 makes use of a blank node representing the location resource. The location resource is not named but specified by its geographic coordinates embraced by square brackets.

3.4.4 RDF Schema

RDF Schema is a vocabulary language for RDF and allows to model vocabularies and ontologies. RDFS describes the logic dependencies among classes, properties, and values. While RDF provides universal means to encode facts about resources and their relationships, RDFS is used to express generic statements about sets of individuals (i.e., classes). RDFS associates resources with classes, states the relations between classes, declares properties, and specifies the domain and range of properties.

Classes in RDFS are much like classes in object oriented programming languages. They allow resources to be defined as instances of classes (by using the property `rdf:type`) and subclasses of classes. Subclass hierarchies can be specified by the RDFS property `rdfs:subClassOf`. The intuitive set theoretic semantics of class instances and subclasses (defined as member-of and subset-of relationships, respectively) ensures the reflexivity and transitivity of `rdfs:subClassOf`. The semantics of RDFS are specified in a W3C Recommendation [31].

Properties can be seen as attributes that are used to describe the resources by assigning values to them. RDF is used to assert property-related statements about objects, and RDFS can extend this capability by defining the class domain and the class range of such properties.

```
1  @prefix rdf: <http://www.w3.org/1999/02/22-rdf-syntax-ns#> .
2  @prefix rdfs: <http://www.w3.org/2000/01/rdf-schema#> .
3  @prefix xsd: <http://www.w3.org/2001/XMLSchema#> .
4  @prefix myims: <http://myitil.org/operation#> .
5  @prefix lss-usdl: <http://w3id.org/lss-usdl/v1#> .
6
7  myims:hasIncidentID rdf:type rdf:Property ;
8    rdfs:subPropertyOf ims:hasID ;
9    rdfs:label "Number required to uniquely identify an incident.
             This number should be used for all reference purpose
             both by internal and external stakeholders."@en ;
10   rdfs:domain myims:IncidentReport ;
11   rdfs:range myims:IncidentID .
12
13 myims:IM_Service lss-usdl:hasGoal myims:Solve_Incident ;
14   myims:implemented "1998-11-23"^^xsd:date .
```

Listing 3.4 Specification of domain and range of properties in RDFS

As the example shown in Listing 3.4 indicates, property hierarchies can be specified with the RDFS property `rdfs:subPropertyOf`. Literals, as shown in line 9 of Listing 3.4, describe data values for properties. A language tag, such as `@en` for English, is used to specify the language of the literal. Data type information can also be appended to literals (see line 14). Each data type is also identified by its URI, which in turn allows applications to interpret their meaning.

Given the logical statement nature of the knowledge represented with ontologies, traditional relational databases are not the ideal storage and query platform for RDFS. Knowledge is represented as sets of subject-predicate-object triples and these are most efficiently stored and accessed in dedicated triple stores, such as Jena TDB[2] and AllegroGraph.[3] Likewise, querying triple stores is done via specific query languages: the current standard language for querying RDF(S) is SPARQL [35].

---

[2] Jena TDB http://jena.apache.org/documentation/tdb/index.html.

[3] AllegroGraph http://www.franz.com/agraph/allegrograph/.

3.4.5 Editors and Validators

Many tools have been developed to support users in modeling structured data, such as RDF and RDFS. Knowledge can be described with the support of ontology modeling tools like Protégé.[4]

A traditional text editor can also be used to create service descriptions, but dedicated applications, such as TextMate for Mac, provide syntax highlighting for Turtle, auto-completion, syntax validation, and format conversions. All helpful features that facilitate the modeling task.

RDF graphs can be validated against a schema and converted to different serialization formats (including RDF/XML, Turtle, and N3) with web-based tools like validators[5, 6] and translators [36].

3.4.6 SPARQL

The RDF information encoded is readable and interpretable by machines, e.g., software programs that utilize the knowledge in applications like a concert ticket selling application. SPARQL is a SQL-like query language that allows to retrieve data from RDF graphs. Answers are computed by matching patterns specified in a query against the given RDF graph.

Basic graph patterns are used in SPARQL queries when a set of triple patterns is matched. Listing 3.5 shows the SPARQL graph pattern query syntax. In SPARQL, Turtle is used to describe the graph patterns. In this example of a query, the set of artists, i.e., the individuals of the class `lss-usdl:ServiceSystem`, are retrieved and returned.

```
1 PREFIX rdf: <http://www.w3.org/1999/02/22-rdf-syntax-ns#>
2 PREFIX lss-usdl: <http://w3id.org/lss-usdl/v1#> .
3
4 SELECT ?service
5 WHERE
6 {
7   ?service rdf:type lss-usdl:ServiceSystem .
8 }
```

Listing 3.5 A SPARQL query to retrieve instances of the class `ServiceSystem`

The answer of `SELECT` queries are bindings for the variables (denoted with a question mark) listed directly after the keyword `SELECT`. In the example, the query results in variable bindings for `?service`, which comprises, as shown in Table 3.2, a list of 3 service systems represented by their URI as used in the RDF graph.

---

[4] Protégé ontology editor and knowledge-base framework http://protege.stanford.edu.

[5] http://www.rdfabout.com/demo/validator/.

[6] http://www.w3.org/RDF/Validator/.

Table 3.2 Results of the SPARQL query shown in Listing 3.5

ServiceSystem
`<http://myitil.org/operation/IM_Service>`
`<http://myitil.org/operation/EM_Service>`
`<http://myitil.org/operation/PM_Service>`

The `IM_Service` was already described. `EM_Service` is the Event Management service, a service to make sure services are constantly monitored, and to filter and categorize events in order to decide on appropriate actions. `PM_Service` is the Problem Management service, a service to manage the lifecycle of all problems and prevent incidents from happening.

Other query forms, e.g., `ASK`, `DESCRIBE`, and `CONSTRUCT`, allow to query for other kind of information. `ASK` returns a boolean answer about the existence of a solution for a specified graph pattern. A `DESCRIBE` query returns an RDF graph describing specified resources.

3.4.7 Linked Data

Linked Data [37] is a subset of the Semantic Web that adheres to the principles of the Semantic Web architecture: commitment to the use of RDF(S) and universal resource identifiers to denote "things". In particular, the following four design principles account for Linked Data:

- Use of URI to name things.
- Use of HTTP URI so that people can lookup the names.
- Lookups on those URI provide further information describing the things in RDF.
- Include links to other URI in the descriptions to allow people to discover further things.

The use of an HTTP URI allows machines and humans to lookup the name and get useful information about resources adhering to the RDF and SPARQL standards. The HyperText Transfer Protocol (HTTP) is prevalently used to exchange data in the web.[7] The use of an HTTP URI further guarantees the uniqueness of the identifier.

The resolvable resource description should contain links to other resource identifiers so that users can discover more things.[8] Linkage comprises external and internal links (for any predicate) and the reuse of external vocabularies, which can be interlinked. The special property `owl:sameAs` specifies the equivalence of different identifiers that refer to the same thing. For example, the Incident Management service is described in different vocabularies or websites. Overlapping data of different sources can be aligned by equivalence statements as illustrated in Listing 3.6.

---

[7] See IEEE RFC2616 at http://tools.ietf.org/html/rfc2616 for details.

[8] Linked Data—Design Issues http://www.w3.org/DesignIssues/LinkedData.

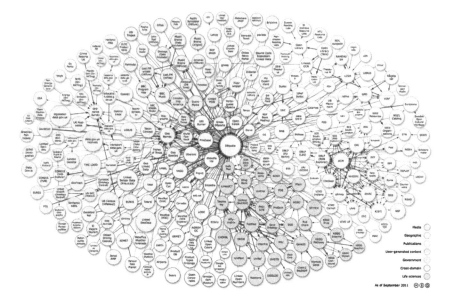

Fig. 3.4 The linked data cloud (http://lod-cloud.net/)

```
1  @prefix owl: <http://www.w3.org/2002/07/owl#> .
2
3  <http://dbpedia.org/resource/Incident_management_(ITSM)> owl:sameAs
       <http://myitil.org/operation/IM_Service> .
```

Listing 3.6 Establishing the equivalence of resources using the property owl:sameAs

Adhering to the Linked Data principles has many advantages in the context of structured representation of data in the web but also in the context of the formal description of service systems. For example, for service search, selection, composition, and analysis.

Figure 3.4 shows a representation of the Linked Data cloud. The figure shows all the knowledge bases available on the web that can be remotely and programmatically accessed. The center of the giant interconnected network is DBpedia, a repository that contains the structured content from the information created as part of the Wikipedia project.

3.5 Model Implementation

Our idea behind the implementation of the 6-point interaction star model is pragmatic and it is based on the objective to create global service systems descriptions using computer-understandable descriptions.

3.5.1 Implementation Details

As explain in Sect. 3.4, the model was implemented as an RDF vocabulary, written in Turtle as opposed to XML due to its better readability [38]. To improve the integration with other semantic web initiatives, the model establishes links with various existing ontologies to reuse concepts from vertical and horizontal domains such as SKOS (taxonomies), Dublin Core (documents), FOAF (people) and so on.

The 6-point interaction star acts as the core of the model. A `ServiceSystem` class was used to group interactions.

A `Role` represents customers, managers, computer agents and so on. We link a role to its respective stakeholders with the property `belongsToBusiness-Entity`. The property connects a `Role` to a `BusinessEntity` of the ontology GoodRelations. This ontology was chosen because it is widely accepted as a valuable Linked Data vocabulary for describing products and services [29].

The class `Process` represents an internal business process of the service system. It is particularly useful to filter interaction flows based on certain processes. Its usefulness can be improved by connecting it to modelled processes. Hence, we link it to a `Process` of the BPMN 2.0 ontology [39]. In future work, connections to different process modeling vocabularies may be considered, to expand the usefulness of this class.

The class `Goal` expresses a motivation for the occurrence of the interaction. This class is not connected to any element of the Linked Data Cloud because its meaning is contained in the context of its service system. Moreover, no relevant ontologies were found that could be used to extend the information of this class.

The class `Location` expresses where an interaction occurs. An instance of this element is connected to another through the property `isLocatedIn` to obtain a hierarchy level. This enables, for instance, associating an interaction with a room and finding that interaction when querying the room. It also has the property `isLocationFrom` that connects it to a `Feature` of the ontology Geonames [40]. This gives an unambiguous geographical context, since a Geonames `Feature` represents any city, country and so on and also uses a hierarchy level.

The concept `Time` gives a temporal context to interactions. It is connected to a `TemporalEntity` of the OWL-Time ontology [41]. This enables a high level of detail for temporal descriptions, such as the date and time of an interaction occurrence by using `DateTimeDescription` or its duration with the concept `DurationDescription`. It is also possible to define temporal relations between interactions by using properties such as `intervalBefore`, `interval Equals` or `intervalAfter`. This enables a lightweight description of a process.

The class `Resource` captures inputs and outputs of the service system. Thus, an interaction can relate to a resource with the property `receivesResource` when it is being introduced from outside the service system; `createsResource` when it is created from within the service system; `consumesResource` when it is consumed from within the service system and `returnsResource` when it is provided to the outside of the service system. A resource is connected to `Quantitative`

Value from the GoodRelations ontology so we may specify quantities. It can also be connected to Resource from DBpedia so that we may give it an unambiguous semantic element, i.e., a resource "Letter" might have an ambiguous meaning by itself (e.g., is it a mail letter or a letter from the alphabet?), but assigning it to a DBpedia Resource gives it an unambiguous semantic value.

As we previously discussed, Interaction and Resource also have subclasses. However, they are not mandatory, and other subclasses may be used instead. That is possible because they are subclasses of Concept from the SKOS ontology [42]. This means that they are concepts that can be extended by concept schemes [43]. Therefore, we can create a ConceptScheme from SKOS for Interaction and another for Resource, create their subclasses and add them to their respective concept schemes through SKOS property hasTopConcept. Similarly, if someone prefers a different set of subclasses, they may create a new concept scheme and assign the new subclasses as top concepts. This capability improves the model's adaptivity and capacity to improve.

Listing 3.7 shows an extract of the RDF code of the LSS-USDL ontology.

```
1  # Every service system is defined by a lss-usdl:ServiceSystem class
2  lss-usdl:ServiceSystem a rdfs:Class, owl:Class;
3      rdfs:label "ServiceSystem" .
4
5  # Every service system features a set of interactions
6  lss-usdl:Interaction a rdfs:Class, owl:Class;
7      rdfs:subClassOf skos:Concept;
8      rdfs:label "Interaction" .
9
10 # Every interaction relates to other entities, such as its location
11 lss-usdl:Location a rdfs:Class, owl:Class;
12     rdfs:label "Location" .
13
14 # This property connects a service system to its interactions
15 lss-usdl:hasInteraction a rdf:Property;
16     rdfs:label "has interaction";
17     rdfs:domain lss-usdl:ServiceSystem;
18     rdfs:range lss-usdl:Interaction .
19
20 # This property connects an interaction to its location
21 lss-usdl:hasLocation a rdf:Property;
22     rdfs:label "has location";
23     rdfs:domain lss-usdl:Interaction;
24     rdfs:range lss-usdl:Location .
25
26 # A location can also be connected to an element of the Geonames
        ontology
27 lss-usdl:isLocationFrom a rdf:Property;
28     rdfs:label "is location from";
29     rdfs:domain lss-usdl:Location;
30     rdfs:range gn:Feature .
```

Listing 3.7 LSS-USDL ontology RDF extract

3.5.2 Integration with the Linked Data Cloud

Another objective, no less important, was to integrate the model with the Linked Data Cloud. This means that the connection between entities of the LSS-USDL model must have a semantic meaning with entities of the LDC. The integration with the LDC is done by reusing relevant Linked Data ontologies, such as Geonames or DBpedia.

The LDC is generating tremendous interest and uptake by researchers and by the industry. The term refers to publicly available data on the World Wide Web in the form of knowledge represented by ontology languages like RDF and OWL, which are established standards by the W3C for metadata sharing and information integration [44].

Historically, corporate information describing data and services was closed inside private databases and "firewall". Linked Data is a recent movement which use Semantic Web advances to enable organizations to give a remote access of their internal data and service assets to others. For example, the US and UK governments already make their legislation available to citizens in a transparent manner using semantic languages. The set of all the datasets made accessible across the world is called the Linked Data Cloud. Driven by researchers, government agencies (e.g., http://govtrack.us and http://legislation.gov.uk), and companies (e.g., The Guardian and The National Library of Germany), the resulting Linked Data alone has grown to over 30 billion RDF triples.

However, in isolation the value of Linked Data is under-explored. By matching vocabularies defined by LSS-USDL and data of the LDC, we will be able to add background knowledge to service systems. For example, this integration enables to execute queries to find information about specific service resources annotated with DBpedia concepts (e.g., passport, medical record, and bill of materials). DBpedia is a repository of structured information retrieved for Wikipedia and accessible as RDF statements. As another example, it also enables to retrieve information, such as the country, population, postal code, and alternative names of the locations where services operate using GeoNames, an ontology with more than 8 million toponyms.

References

1. Stephen Vargo and Robert Lusch. Evolving to a new marketing dominant logic for marketing. *Journal of Marketing,* 68(1):1–17, 2004.
2. Scott Sampson and Craig Froehle. Foundations and implications of a proposed unified services theory. *Production and Operations Management,* 15(2):329–343, 2006.
3. Steven Alter. Work system theory: Overview of core concepts, extensions, and challenges for the future. *Journal of the Association for Information Systems,* 14(2), 2013.
4. Rainer Alt and Hans-Dieter Zimmermann. Preface: introduction to special section-business models. *Electronic Markets,* 11(1):3–9, 2001.
5. Otto Petrovic, Christian Kittl, and Ryan Teksten. Developing business models for ebusiness. *Available at SSRN* 1658505, 2001.

6. Maya Kaner and Reuven Karni. Design of service systems using a knowledge-based approach. *Knowledge and Process Management*, 14(4):260–274, 2007.

7. Reuven Karni and Maya Kaner. An engineering tool for the conceptual design of service systems. *Advances in Services Innovations*, pages 65–83, 2007.

8. Reuven Karni and Maya Kaner. Teaching innovative conceptual design of systems in the service sector. *Technological Forecasting and Social Change*, 64(2):225–240, 2000.

9. Sybren Kinderen and Jaap Gordijn. e3service: An ontological approach for deriving multi-supplier IT-service bundles from consumer needs. In *Proceedings of the 41st annual Hawaii international conference on system sciences*, 2008.

10. Sybren Kinderen and Jaap Gordijn. Reasoning about substitute choices and preference ordering in e-services. In *Advanced Information Systems Engineering*, pages 390–404. Springer, 2008.

11. Jim Spohrer and Paul Maglio. Service science: Toward a smarter planet. *Introduction to service engineering*, pages 3–30, 2009.

12. Alexander Osterwalder and Yves Pigneur. *Business model generation: a handbook for visionaries, game changers, and challengers*. Wiley, 2010.

13. Erwin Fielt. An Extended Business Model Canvas for Co-Creation and Partnering, 2010.

14. Erwin Fielt. To what extent is the Business Model Canvas constraining? A Co-Creation Canvas example. http://fieltnotes.blogspot.pt/2010/11/to-what-extent-is-business-model-canvas.html, 2010

15. Erwin Fielt. Alternative business model canvasses: A Partnering Canvas example. http://fieltnotes.blogspot.pt/2010/12/alternative-business-model-canvasses.html, 2010

16. Andreas Zolnowski, Martin Semmann, and Tilo Böhmann. Introducing a Co-Creation Perspective to Service Business Models. In *Enterprise Modelling and Information Systems Architectures (EMISA)*, page 243, 2011.

17. Paul Maglio, Stephen Vargo, Nathan Caswell, and Jim Spohrer. The service system is the basic abstraction of service science. *Information Systems and e-business Management*, 7(4):395–406, 2009.

18. Lynn Shostack. Designing services that deliver. *Harvard Business Review*, 62(1):133–139, 1984.

19. Kevin Barnhurst and Diana Mutz. American journalism and the decline in event-centered reporting. *Journal of Communication*, 47(4):27–53, 1997.

20. John Zachman. Enterprise architecture: The issue of the century. *Database Programming and Design*, 10(3):44–53, 1997.

21. Andrew Blair, John Debenham, and Jenny Edwards. Requirements analysis for intelligent decision support systems. In *Intelligent Information Systems, 1994. Proceedings of the 1994 Second Australian and New Zealand Conference on*, pages 482–486. IEEE, 1994.

22. Marlon Dumas, Justin O'Sullivan, Mitra Heravizadeh, David Edmond, and Arthur ter Hofstede. Towards a semantic framework for service description. In Robert Meersman, Karl Aberer, and Tharam Dillon, editors, DS-9, volume 239 of *IFIP Conference Proceedings*, pages 277–291. Kluwer, 2001.

23. Eva Söderström, Birger Andersson, Paul Johannesson, Erik Perjons, and Benkt Wangler. Towards a framework for comparing process modelling languages. In *Advanced Information Systems Engineering*, pages 600–611. Springer, 2006.

24. Alistair Barros, Uwe Kylau, and Daniel Oberle. Unified Service Description Language 3.0 (USDL) Overview, 2011.

25. Sabine Fließ and Michael Kleinaltenkamp. Blueprinting the service company: Managing service processes efficiently. *Journal of Business Research*, 57(4):392–404, 2004.

26. Holger Luczak, Christian Gill, and Bernhard Sander. Architecture for Service Engineering The Design and Development of Industrial Service Work. In Dieter Spath and Klaus-Peter Fähnrich, editors, *Advances in Services Innovations*, pages 47–63. Springer, Berlin Heidelberg, 2007.

27. Claudio Masolo, Stefano Borgo, Aldo Gangemi, Nicola Guarino, and Alessandro Oltramari. WonderWeb Deliverable D18, Ontology Library *(final)*. *ICT Project*, 33052, 2003.

28. Geert Poels. The resource-service-system model for service science. In *Advances in Conceptual Modeling-Applications and Challenges*, pages 117–126. Springer, 2010.

29. Tom Heath and Christian Bizer. Linked data: Evolving the web into a global data space. *Synthesis lectures on the semantic web: theory and technology*, 1(1):1–136, 2011.
30. Frank Manola and Eric Miller. RDF primer. W3C recommendation, W3C, February 2004. accessed Aug. 15, 2013.
31. Dan Brickley and Ramanathan Guha. RDF vocabulary description language 1.0: RDF Schema. W3C recommendation, W3C, February 2004. accessed Aug. 15, 2013.
32. Dean Allemang and James Hendler. *Semantic Web for the Working Ontologist: Effective Modeling in RDFS and OWL*. Morgan Kaufmann Publishers Inc., San Francisco, CA, USA, 2011.
33. Tim Bray, Jean Paoli, Michael Sperberg-McQueen, Eve Maler, and François Yergeau. Extensible markup language (XML) 1.1 (second edition). W3C recommendation, W3C, September 2006. accessed Aug. 15, 2013.
34. David Beckett and Tim Berners-Lee. Turtle - terse RDF triple language. W3C team submission, W3C, March 2011. accessed Aug. 15, 2013.
35. W3C SPARQL Working Group. SPARQL 1.1 overview. W3C recommendation, W3C, March 2013. accessed Aug. 15, 2013.
36. Alex Stolz, Bene Rodriguez-Castro, and Martin Hepp. RDF translator: A restful multi-format data converter for the semantic web. Technical Report TR-2013-1, Universität der Bundeswehr München, July 2013.
37. Christian Bizer, Tom Heath, and Tim Berners-Lee. Linked Data - The Story So Far. *International Journal on Semantic Web and Information Systems*, 5(3):1–22, 2009.
38. David Beckett and Tim Berners-Lee. Turtle-terse RDF triple language. *W3C Team Submission*, 14, 2008.
39. Christine Natschläger. Towards a BPMN 2.0 Ontology. In *Business Process Model and Notation*, pages 1–15. Springer, 2011.
40. Bernard Vatant and Marc Wick. Geonames ontology. http://www.geonames.org/ontology, 2012. Accessed at 31/05/2013
41. Jerry Hobbs and Feng Pan. Time ontology in OWL. *W3C working draft*, 27, 2006.
42. Antoine Isaac and Ed Summers. SKOS Simple Knowledge Organization System Primer. W3C Working Group Note. *World Wide Web Consortium*, 2009.
43. Alistair Miles, Brian Matthews, Michael Wilson, and Dan Brickley. SKOS core: simple knowledge organisation for the web. In *International Conference on Dublin Core and Metadata Applications*, 2005.
44. Jorge Cardoso. *The Syntactic and the Semantic* Web, pages 1–23. IGI Global, 2007.

Chapter 4
Modeling and Programming

This chapter explains how a service system can be modeled with LSS-USDL using semantic web languages and technologies, how it can be accessed and queried programmatically, and how it can be annotated with background knowledge from the Linked Data cloud. The service system modeled, the Incident Management (IM) service, was selected from the Information Technology Infrastructure Library (ITIL) since this set of best practices for IT service management, that focuses on aligning IT services with the needs of business, is being widely adopted by large enterprises. The programming language used was Python because stable software libraries to access and modify RDF models are available and because it is a widely used general-purpose, high-level language with an emphasis on code readability. Finally, we have selected DBpedia from the Linked Data cloud as a repository of background knowledge to annotate the service system modeled since it is one of the largest existing knowledge bases.

4.1 ITIL

The Information Technology Infrastructure Library (ITIL) [1] is commonly used in the industry for IT service management. ITIL provides a set of best practices which take often the form of reference models and accepted processes which are sound and efficient. The adoption of reference models is generally motivated by the following reasons [2]:

Design. They significantly speed up the design of process models by providing reusable and high quality content.

Optimization. They optimize the design as they have been developed over a long period and usually capture the business insight of experts.

Compliance. They ease the compliance with industry regulations and requirements and, thus, mitigate risk.

© The Author(s) 2014
J. Cardoso et al., *Service Systems*,
SpringerBriefs in Computer Science, DOI 10.1007/978-3-319-10813-1_4

Alignment. They are an essential mean to create a link to align business needs and IT service implementations.

Worldwide, many well-known companies are adopting ITIL for IT service management. Examples include large software providers such as Microsoft, HP, and IBM; financial services societies such as Bank of America, Deutsche Bank, and Barclays Bank; manufacturers such as Boeing, Caterpillar, Toyota, and Bombardier; and departments of defence such as the US Army, US Navy, and US Air Force. As a concrete example of cost reduction, Proctor and Gamble reduced IT spendings in 10 percent of their annual IT budget ($125M) by adopting ITIL. The speed-up and optimization of services were the main reasons behind the savings.

4.1.1 The ITIL Lifecycle

ITIL consists of five main books: service strategy, service design, service transition, service operation, and continual service improvement. An introductory book to ITIL service management is also available. Each of the five main volumes is structured, making the interpretation and cross referencing easier. They textually describe the best practices that can be followed by a company to manage IT services. ITIL should not be viewed as a piece of code, system, or software application. The five phases of the lifecycle have the following characteristics:

Service Strategy provides guidance on the principles of service management that support the development of policies and processes across the ITIL service life cycle. Topics include service portfolios and implementation of strategy.

Service Design provides guidance for the development of services using design principles and methods for converting strategic objectives into portfolios of services. It is also concerned with service levels, and conformance to standards and regulations.

Service Transition aims at introducing services into live operation in a systematic and controlled manner by ensuring that the transition processes are streamlined, effective and efficient, minimize risks of delays, and guaranty established quality levels.

Service Operation provides best-practice advice and guidance to deliver and support services. It manages service providers' performance and customer requirements. Key services include event management and incident management.

Continual Service Improvement aligns IT services to changing business needs by identifying and implementing improvements. Important activities include analyzing service level results and implementing activities to improve the quality, efficiency, and effectiveness of services offered.

This chapter will look into the service operation phase, and, more precisely, it will model the incident management service.

4.1.2 The Incident Management Service

The primary objective of the Incident Management (IM) service is to resolve incidents (e.g., application bugs, disks-usage thresholds exceeded, or printers not working) in the quickest and most effective possible way. If a user cannot print, he contacts the Service Desk for help which creates a record describing the incident. If the issue cannot be resolved immediately, the Service Desk manager opens an incident which is assigned to a technician. When the technician finds the cause of the problem, he fixes the problem and closes the incident. The Service Desk manager informs the user to retry to print. If the user can print, the Service Desk manager closes the incident. Otherwise, the Service Desk reopens the incident record.

Figure 4.1 provides a simple representation of the business process model behind the IM service. A set of activities such as Incident Identification,

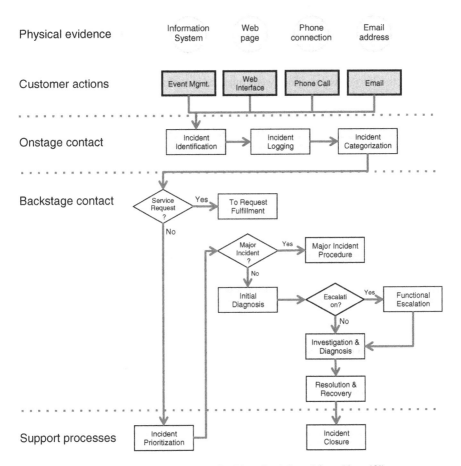

Fig. 4.1 The ITIL Incident Management service blueprint (adapted from [4, p. 48])

Incident logging, and Incident Prioritization are orchestrated to solve an incident using a proven process.

While nowadays software solutions which provide ITIL services already exist (e.g., ServiceDesk Plus and Aegis Help Desk), our objective is not to develop similar systems or provide a more or less functional alternative. Our goal is to demonstrate how the IM service can be modeled with LSS-USDL.

4.2 Step-by-Step Modeling

After understanding the ITIL Incident Management service and the main concepts behind the Semantic Web, the major task is to model the IM service using the LSS-USDL model.

ITIL reference models provide valuable recommendations for the implementation of services. However, each company is free to customize an implementation based on the specificities of their business. Therefore, companies adopting ITIL can improve their implementations by using theoretical, methodological, and technical contributions from service science.

The methodology we have followed consisted in looking at the IM service as a flow of interactions and using the LSS-USDL model to capture each interaction. In order words, each interaction was analyzed by answering the questions: *who*, *why*, *where*, *when*, *what*, and *how*. The answers to these questions provided detailed information about the more relevant interactions features, such as: roles, goals, locations, time, resources, and processes, completing the model information.

4.2.1 Prefixes and External Vocabularies

The modeling exercise with Turtle and using the LSS-USDL model begins by specifying a set of prefixes. Prefixes are a convenient method for representing a namespace URI with a short string. Prefixes facilitate the reference to other ontologies in an easy and unambiguous way. Each prefix refers to a basilar ontology which is used to model the IM service. Listing 4.1 shows the prefixes used to model the IM service. For example, Lines 2 and 7 define unique namespaces for the RDF Schema and the Friend of a Friend namespace vocabulary, perspectively. When we need to reference entities from those two schemata, we can just use the short prefix instead of the full URI.

```
1  @prefix : <http://myitil.org/operations#>.
2  @prefix rdf: <http://www.w3.org/1999/02/22-rdf-syntax-ns#>.
3  @prefix rdfs: <http://www.w3.org/2000/01/rdf-schema#>.
4  @prefix owl: <http://www.w3.org/2002/07/owl#>.
5  @prefix xsd: <http://www.w3.org/2001/XMLSchema#>.
6  @prefix gr: <http://purl.org/goodrelations/v1#>.
```

```
7 @prefix foaf: <http://xmlns.com/foaf/0.1/>.
8 @prefix time: <http://www.w3.org/2006/time#>.
9 @prefix lss-usdl: <http://w3id.org/lss-usdl/v1#>.
```

Listing 4.1 Prefixes and external vocabularies

There are some common ontologies used by many models or instances that we have also used. For example, the W3C ontologies: rdf, rdfs, owl, and xml. The most specialized ontologies we have used are:

- GoodRelations[1] (gr) [3] references the GoodRelations ontology, a standardized vocabulary to describe product, price, store, and company data.
- Friend of a friend (foaf)[2] is an ontology describing persons, their activities, and their relations to other people and objects.
- Time Ontology (time)[3] covers basic temporal relations. The ontology allows to capture temporal relationships such as before and during.

The use of external vocabularies and ontologies enables to integrate the IM service instance to a large base of knowledge made available by many organizations and initiatives.

4.2.2 The Service System

As a first step to build our IM service instance, we define a new service system named IncidentManagementService. It is a new class that inherits all the properties of the class lss-usdl:ServiceSystem. To provide descriptive information to this new service, we used the RDFS predicates label, comments, and the LSS-USDL term hasGoal. See lines 1–4 of Listing 4.2.

The incident management service handles incidents (e.g., failures, questions, or queries reported by users) and consists of the following steps:

1. Identification
2. Logging
3. Classification
4. Prioritization
5. Diagnosis
6. Escalation
7. Investigation and diagnosis
8. Resolution and recovery
9. Closure

---

[1] http://purl.org/goodrelations/.

[2] http://xmlns.com/foaf/0.1/.

[3] http://www.w3.org/TR/owl-time.

Steps were captured as `Interaction` with the predicate `hasInteraction`
(Listing 4.2, lines 6–14). The names of the steps recommended by ITIL were slightly
changed to more meaningful while reading the Turtle statements.

```
 1  :IncidentManagementService a lss-usdl:ServiceSystem ;
 2    rdfs:label "ITIL Incident Management Service";
 3    rdfs:comment"A service system for Incident Management, based on
              ITIL specs. The main objective of the incident management
              process is to resume the regular state of affairs as quickly
              as possible and minimize the impact on business processes." ;
 4    lss-usdl:hasGoal :SolveIncident ;
 5
 6    lss-usdl:hasInteraction
 7      :IncidentIdentification ,
 8      :IncidentLogging ,
 9      :IncidentClassification ,
10      :IncidentPrioritization ,
11      :InitialDiagnosis ,
12      :IncidentEscalation ,
13      :InvestigationDiagnosis ,
14      :ResolutionRecovery ,
15      :IncidentClosure .
```

Listing 4.2 The first building block to construct a service system

The following sections will detail how each interaction was modeled.

4.2.3 Interactions

Since there are 9 interactions, we will only describe two of them, which is sufficient
to illustrate how modeling is performed: `IncidentLogging` and `Initial
Diagnosis`. The complete specification of the interactions can be found at http://
eden.dei.uc.pt/~jcardoso/rdf/lss-usdl-eg/ITIL_IM_service.ttl. Each interaction answers to six questions: *who* (roles), *why* (goals), *where* (locations), *what* (resources),
when (time), and *how* (processes).

4.2.3.1 Incident Logging

Essential step in managing incidents is to receive and record them. This is carried
out by the Incident Logging interaction. When it is determined that an incident has
occurred through a Service Desk telephone call or automatically detected via an event
alert, the logging interaction will document the incident. All relevant information
describing the incident must be logged so that a full historical record is main-
tained. Logging should at a minimum record the date and time of the incident, the
person/system reporting the incident, and a description of the problem. Listing 4.3
shows the complete specification for this interaction.

```
1  :IncidentLogging a lss-usdl:BackstageInteraction ;
2      rdfs:label "An incident is logged";
3      rdfs:comment"Incidents reported to the Service Desk must be
            logged with the date and time stamp when they were
            generated." ;
4
5      lss-usdl:performedBy :ServiceDeskManager ;
6      lss-usdl:hasGoal :DealWithReportedIncident ;
7      lss-usdl:hasLocation :ABCompany ;
8      lss-usdl:belongsToProcess :ITServiceIncidentManagement ;
9      lss-usdl:consumesResource :ReportData ;
10     lss-usdl:consumesResource :IncidentData ;
11     lss-usdl:createsResource :IncidentID ;
12     lss-usdl:createsResource :IncidentRecord .
13
14     lss-usdl:hasTime
15         [a lss-usdl:Time ;
16             lss-usdl:hasTemporalEntity :IncidentLoggingTime] ;
17
18 :IncidentLoggingTime a time:ProperInterval ;
19     time:intervalAfter :IncidentIdentificationTime ;
20     time:intervalBefore :IncidentCategorizationTime .
```

Listing 4.3 The Incident Identification interaction

The example illustrates that the interaction is described as a Backstage Interaction, which is performed by the ServiceDeskManager role; it has the DealWithReportedIncident goal; it is performed at the ABCompany location; it belongs to the ITServiceIncidentManagement process; it consumes two knowledge resources (IncidentData and ReportData) and it creates two (IncidentID and IncidentRecord). The interaction has also a temporal entity associated which allows specifying that this interaction occurs before the IncidentCategorization interaction and after the Incident Identification interaction.

The knowledge resources IncidentData and ReportData typically include the following information:

- Basic information needed to handle the incident, such as date and time of the occurrence, description of the incident, and systems affected.
- Supporting information for the resolution of the incident that may be asked to the submitter using, possibly, a specific form.

The IncidentRecord will aggregate these information and will assign a reference to the incident to uniquely identify it in both internal processes and when communicating with the person affected by the incident.

4.2.3.2 Initial Diagnosis

The Initial Diagnosis is the fourth step in the incident management process. It follows
the incident categorization. The initial diagnosis is the first attempt at resolving an
incident. Typically, the technical staff of the Service Desk will carry out an initial
diagnosis and will try to understand the incident being reported. He will try to discover
the full symptoms of the incident, determine what went wrong, and how to solve the
problem. If available, diagnostic scripts and known error information is valuable in
allowing an earlier and accurate diagnosis. The interaction described in Listing 4.4
represents the initial diagnosis of an incident performed by the technical staff of the
Service Desk.

```
1  :InitialDiagnosis a lss-usdl:BackstageInteraction ;
2     rdfs:label "An initial diagnosis for the incident is performed";
3     rdfs:comment"The initial diagnosis of incidents is mainly a
             human process. The Service Desk technical staff looks at the
             information within the incident and communicates with the
             user to diagnose the problem." ;
4
5  lss-usdl:performedBy :TechnicalStaff ;
6     lss-usdl:hasGoal :HandleIncident ;
7     lss-usdl:hasTime [a lss-usdl:Time ;
8        lss-usdl:hasTemporalEntity :InitialDiagnosisTime] ;
9     lss-usdl:hasLocation :ABCompany ;
10    lss-usdl:belongsToProcess :ITServiceIncidentManagement ;
11    lss-usdl:consumesResource :IncidentRecord .
12
13 :IncidentInitialDiagnosisTime a time:ProperInterval ;
14    time:intervalAfter :DetermineIfIncidentIsMajorTime ;
15    time:intervalBefore :DetermineIfFunctionalScalationIsNeededTime
             .
```

Listing 4.4 The Initial Diagnosis

The interaction is described as a `BackstageInteraction` which is performed by the `ServiceDeskStaff` role; it has the `HandleIncident` goal; it
is performed at the `ABCompany` location; it belongs to the `ITServiceIncident`
`Management` process and it consumes the knowledge resource `Incident`
`Report`. The interaction has also a temporal entity associated, which allows specifying that it occurs before the `DetermineIfFuntionalScalationIsNeeded`
`Time` interaction and after the `DetermineIfIncidentIsMajorTime` interaction.

4.2.4 Roles

Each interaction has a `performedBy` predicate indicating *who* is participating in
the interaction. In some cases, there are many roles for the same interaction. Roles

can belong to an entity. In such a case, the concept Business Entities from GoodRela-tions is used. While the number of roles depends on the ITIL implementation that a company chooses to make, we have compiled a list of 5 roles which are typical:

Service Desk Manager. Functions as the primary point of contact for incidents reported from users. The role owns the results of the service desk function.

Problem Manager. Responsible for managing the lifecycle of all problems. The primary objectives are to prevent incidents from happening and to minimize the impact of incidents that cannot be prevented.

Incident Manager. The role assigned to the person who owns the results of the Incident Management service and of its effective implementation.

Technical Staff. Aggregates the first, second, and third-tier support groups, including specialist support groups and external service providers.

End User. The end users and employees of a company that experience difficulties with IT and which rely on services to restore a normal processing as quickly as possible after an incident has occurred.

Listing 4.5 describes these roles using the LSS-USDL model. Each role has a label and a brief description as well as an assignment to a business entity it belongs to. Most of the roles belong to the ABCompany company, except the role `ProblemManager` which belong to the `ExtCompany` company.

```
1  :ServiceDeskManager a lss-usdl:Role ;
2     rdfs:label "Service Desk Manager";
3     rdfs:comment"Functions as the primary point of contact for
          incidents reported from users.";
4     lss-usdl:belongsToBusinessEntity :ABCompany.
5
6  :ProblemManager a lss-usdl:Role ;
7     rdfs:label"Problem Manager";
8     rdfs:comment"Responsible for managing the lifecycle of all
          problems.";
9     lss-usdl:belongsToBusinessEntity :ExtCompany .
10
11 :IncidentManager a lss-usdl:Role ;
12    rdfs:label"Incident Manager";
13    rdfs:comment"The person who owns the results of the Incident
          Management service";
14   lss-usdl:belongsToBusinessEntity :ABCompany .
15
16 :TechnicalStaff a lss-usdl:Role ;
17    rdfs:label"Technical Staff";
18    rdfs:comment"Support technical staff";
19    lss-usdl:belongsToBusinessEntity :ABCCompany .
20
21 :EndUser a lss-usdl:Role ;
22    rdfs:label"End User";
23    rdfs:comment"The end users and employees of a company that
          experience difficulties with IT." ;
24    lss-usdl:belongsToBusinessEntity :ABCompany .
```

Listing 4.5 Modeling roles and business entities

Not all the roles defined were used in the examples of this chapter. The objective was to show how role modeling can be achieved. To structure and organize the many roles that can exist, the knowledge organization systems SKOS[4] can be used to construct a classification schema or a taxonomy.

4.2.5 Goals

The concept of goal has been used in many domains such as business sciences and strategic planning. The objective is to provide a planning framework which links goals with interactions. It is intended to assist ITIL service owners in understanding the effects of interactions on services.

Each interaction has a one, or more, hasGoal predicate(s), indicating the goal(s) a specific interaction occurs. Listing 4.6 shows examples of several goals.

```
1   :ReportIncident a lss-usdl:Goal ;
2       rdfs:label "Report Incident";
3       rdfs:comment"A user, technical staff or system reports an
            incident regarding an IT service.".
4
5   :HandleIncident a lss-usdl:Goal ;
6       rdfs:label"Handle Incident";
7       rdfs:comment"Execute several actions to deal with a reported
            incident.".
8
9   :RestoreNormalOperation a lss-usdl:Goal ;
10      rdfs:label"Restore Operation";
11      rdfs:comment"Restore the normal service operation as quickly as
            possible." .
```

Listing 4.6 Modeling the goals of interactions

Since goals are targets for achievements, they should be written in such a way that they express the rationale for the interactions that exist and guides decisions at various levels within the enterprise. Here again, the SKOS can be used to organize goals using, e.g., structured controlled vocabularies.

4.2.6 Locations

The class lss-usdl:Location is concerned with the geographical location of the IM service interactions. Locations can be expressed simply as a list of the places where interactions occur, or they can take a more detailed form by describing how locations are related or detailing the facilities/IT that are available in each location.

---

[4] http://www.w3.org/2004/02/skos/.

Each interaction has a `hasLocation` predicate indicating where the interaction happens. For the IM service, we have identified two locations: the `ServiceDesk Office` and the `UserOffice`. The `ServiceDeskOffice` represents the location where a user or system can report an incident and the `UserOffice` location refers to the location where the company staff is working.

```
1  :ServiceDeskOffice a lss-usdl:Location ;
2    rdfs:label "Service Desk Office".
3
4  :UserOffice a lss-usdl:Location ;
5    rdfs:label"User Office" .
```

Listing 4.7 Modeling locations within a service system

The Listing 4.7 shows the definition of both locations. While these locations are concepts that only have a meaning for the company implementing the IM service, another approach to use geographical descriptions. This can be achieved by using, e.g., the GeoNames ontology,[5] a data structure containing over 8.5 million geographical names. The information covers coordinates, administrative divisions, postal codes, amongst others. GeoNames can answer questions such as what are the coordinates for a location; which region or province does a location belong to; and what city or address is near a given GPS latitude/longitude.

4.2.7 Time

Each interaction uses a `hasTime` predicate to indicate when it occurs. The Time ontology is used for temporal reasoning. Typically, two time modeling options can be defined. The first one, used in this example, defines temporal relationships between interactions using constructs such as before or after. The second, uses time intervals of times point to define when an interaction can occur or occurs. Listing 4.8 exemplifies the use of the concept `ProperInterval` to describe the temporal dependencies between interactions.

```
1  :IncidentIdentificationTime a time:ProperInterval;
2    time:intervalAfter :IncidentCategorizationTime .
3
4  :IncidentCategorizationTime a time:ProperInterval;
5    time:intervalBefore :IncidentIdentificationTime;
6    time:intervalAfter :IncidentPrioritizationTime .
7
8  :IncidentPrioritizationTime a time:ProperInterval;
9    time:intervalBefore :IncidentCategorization;
10   time:intervalAfter :InitialDiagnosisTime .
11
12 :InitialDiagnosisTime a time:ProperInterval;
13   time:intervalBefore :IncidentPrioritizationTime;
```

---

[5] http://www.geonames.org/.

```
14     time:intervalAfter :InvestigationDiagnosisTime .
15
16  :InvestigationDiagnosisTime a time:ProperInterval;
17     time:intervalBefore :InitialDiagnosisTime;
18     time:intervalAfter :ResolutionRecoveryTime;
19     time:intervalEquals :scalationFirstTime .
20
21  :ResolutionRecoveryTime a time:ProperInterval;
22     time:intervalBefore :InvestigationDiagnosisTime;
23     time:intervalAfter :IncidentClosureTime;
24     time:intervalEquals :scalationSecondTime .
25
26  :IncidentClosureTime a time:ProperInterval;
27     time:intervalBefore :ResolutionRecoveryTime.
28
29  :scalationFirstTime a time:TemporalEntity;
30     rdfs:label "Scalation time for first level";
31     rdfs:comment"Need to define hasDurationDescription".
32
33  :scalationSecondTime a time:TemporalEntity;
34     rdfs:label"Scalation time for second level";
35     rdfs:comment"Need to define hasDurationDescription" .
```

Listing 4.8 Modeling time within a service system

The example uses the `intervalAfter` and `intervalBefore` predicates to define the sequence of interactions according to the process model from Fig. 4.1.

4.2.8 Resources

Interactions can use the `receivesResource`, `consumesResource`, `createsResource`, or `returnsResource` predicate to indicate the resources received, consumed, created, or returned. For the IM service, we have defined that the interaction `IncidentLogging` consumes knowledge from the user in the form of `ReportData` and `IncidentData` and creates two new resources: `IncidentID` and `IncidentRecord`. Listing 4.9 defines the resource `IncidentRecord`.

```
1  :IncidentRecord a lss-usdl:KnowledgeResource ;
2     rdfs:label "Incident Record";
3     rdfs:comment"An Incident Record generated during the
            IncidentLogging" ;
4     owl:sameAs dbpediar:Incident_report .
5
6  :Severity a rdf:Property ;
7     rdfs:domain :IncidentRecord ;
8     rdfs:range xsd:integer  .
```

Listing 4.9 Modeling the resources associated with interactions

Naturally, the `IncidentRecord` should include more fields, besides `Severity`, to reflect the complexity of records, which describe an incident. Our example is simple to convey the principle of resource and their descriptions.

4.2.9 Process

Each interaction belongs to a business process model (concept), which can be specified using the property `belongsToProcess` (see Listing 4.3). In turn, the process model can be associated with an implementation, which can be made using, e.g., the Business Process Modeling Notation (BPMN) or Event-driven Process Chain (EPC) notations.

```
1  :ITServiceIncidentManagement a lss-usdl:Process ;
2     rdfs:label "Incident Management Business Process Model" ;
3     lss-usdl:hasBPMN bpmnrep:IM_BPMN .
```

Listing 4.10 Modeling the process to which interactions belong

Listing 4.10 shows a process model `ITServiceIncidentManagement` created to exemplify the use of the property `hasBPMN` to associate an implementation with the model, which, in this case, can be accessed at `bpmnrep:IM_BPMN`. While LSS-USDL only includes one property to attach BPMN processes to a service system, this was done as a proof of concept and additional properties can be specified to relate interactions with other process modeling languages.

4.3 Programming with LSS-USDL

Since many open source semantic web libraries and tools are available to store, reason, and define rules and queries against RDF graphs, we will use this programming language to illustrate how LSS-USDL instances can be managed programmatically.

This section will provide programming examples which rely on two main libraries:

- RDFLib.[6] A library for working with RDF graphs.
- SPARQLWrapper.[7] A wrapper around a SPARQL service to help in creating a query.

Several good books have been written in the field of semantic web and can be read to complement this section, e.g., Toby Segaran's book on Programming the Semantic Web, which has many programming examples in Python.

---

[6] MacOS user can use the following command to install RDFLib: `sudo pip install rdflib`. Command also available for other UNIX-based OSs, such as Linux.

[7] The following command can be used to install SPARQLWrapper: `sudo pip install SPARQLWrapper`.

4.3.1 Using RDFLib

The first exercise consists in using the RDFLib to load the LSS-USDL instance of the IM service modeled in the previous section and print the main characteristics of the underlying service system. Listing 4.11 shows our example.

Before using RDFLib, it is necessary to add some import declarations (line 1): URIRef, Namespace, Graph, RDF, RDFS. We will assume that the LSS-USDL service system instance is stored in the file ITIL_IM_service.ttl. A Graph object is used to load and parse the service system definition. This object will enable to gain access to methods to travel thought the graph and inspect each node and edge. The constructor Namespace enables to create prefixes.

RDFLib graphs support basic triple (subject, predicate, object) pattern matching by using the triples() function. This function returns triples that match the pattern given as argument. In our example, since we were not interested in whole triples, we used the methods subjects(), objects(), and subject_objects(). Each function takes parameters for the components of the triple to constraint. Listing 4.11 shows an example.

```
 1  from rdflib import URIRef, Namespace, Graph, RDF, RDFS
 2
 3  g = Graph()
 4  g.parse("file:ITIL_IM_service.ttl", format='n3')
 5  lss_usdl = Namespace("http://w3id.org/lss-usdl/v1#")
 6
 7  print("\n--- Service System ---")
 8  for lss in g.subjects(RDF.type, URIRef(lss_usdl['ServiceSystem'])):
 9      print"Name:", lss.rsplit("#", 2)[1]
10      for ss_description in g.objects(lss, RDFS.comment):
11          print"Description:", ss_description
12
13  print"\n--- Interaction Points: ---"
14  for sub, obj in
         g.subject_objects(URIRef(lss_usdl['hasInteraction'])):
15      ss_interaction = obj.rsplit("#", 2)[1]
16      print ss_interaction
```

Listing 4.11 Loading and printing the characteristics of an LSS-USDL instance

Lines 7–11 retrieve all the triples with the predicate RDF.type and the object ServiceSystem. This entails to retrieve all the service systems specified in the Turtle file loaded. Lines 13–16 retrieve all the triples with the predicate hasInteraction, which are then printed. This corresponds to retrieving all the interaction points.

Listing 4.12 shows the output printed to the console.

```
 1 --- Service System ---
 2 Name: IMService
 3 Description: A service system for Incident Management, based on ITIL
         specs. The main objective of the incident management process
         is to resume the regular state of affairs as quickly as
         possible and minimize the impact on business processes.
 4
 5 --- Interaction Points: ---
 6 ResolutionRecovery
 7 IncidentCategorization
 8 IncidentClosure
 9 IncidentIdentification
10 IncidentPrioritization
11 IncidentEscalation
12 InitialDiagnosis
13 IncidentLogging
14 InvestigationDiagnosis
```

Listing 4.12 The output of Listing 4.11 printed to the console

The interaction points are parsed in a random fashion. To consider temporal dependencies, the temporal relations specified in Sect. 4.2.7 would need to be accounted for.

4.3.2 SPARQL Queries

While the previous section explained how to access information stored in a service system, the programming steps needed are usually many and the logic of the information retrieved is hidden within the code. Therefore, the use of a query language to retrieve information is always a good decision. SPARQL queries allow to ask specific queries to the graph using a SQL like syntax.

In nutshell, SPARQL queries have a SELECT and WHERE clause, similarly to SQL, a PREFIX declaration can be used to facilitate the use of URIs, similarly to the Turtle language. The query results are returned as an array of rows, which can be easily inspected using Phyton methods to traverse the collection of rows and tuples assignment.

Listing 4.13 shows how to determine the roles associates with the interactions of the IM service.

```
 1 from rdflib import Namespace, Graph, RDF, URIRef, RDFS
 2
 3 g = Graph()
 4 g.parse("file:ITIL_IM_service.ttl", format='n3')
 5 lss_usdl = Namespace("http://w3id.org/lss-usdl/v1#")
 6
 7 qres = g.query(
 8   '''''PREFIX lss-usdl: <http://w3id.org/lss-usdl/v1#>
 9     SELECT DISTINCT ?lss ?interaction ?role
```

```
10      WHERE {
11          ?lss lss-usdl:hasInteraction ?interaction .
12          ?interaction lss-usdl:performedBy ?role .
13      }""")
14
15 print"\n--- Interaction Roles ---"
16 for row in qres:
17      lss, interaction, role = row
18      l = lss.rsplit("#", 2)[1]
19      r = role.rsplit("#", 2)[1]
20      i = interaction.rsplit("#", 2)[1]
21      print"Interaction"+ l +"/"+ i +"has role" + r
```

Listing 4.13 Querying a service system to obtain information on interactions and roles

The query is constructed in lines 7–13 and lines 16–21 show how to iterate through the results to retrieve the information need to display in the console.

Listing 4.14 shows another example, which is interesting since it queries a service system to determine the last(s) interactions that are executed. This requires to use the Time ontology.

```
1 from rdflib import Namespace, Graph, RDF, URIRef, RDFS
2
3 g = Graph()
4 g.parse("file:ITIL_IM_service.ttl", format='n3')
5 lss_usdl = Namespace("http://w3id.org/lss-usdl/v1#")
6
7 qres = g.query(
8   ''''''PREFIX lss-usdl: <http://w3id.org/lss-usdl/v1#>
9      PREFIX time: <http://www.w3.org/2006/time#>
10      SELECT DISTINCT ?lss ?interaction
11      WHERE {
12          ?lss lss-usdl:hasInteraction ?interaction .
13          ?interaction lss-usdl:hasTime ?time .
14          ?time lss-usdl:hasTemporalEntity ?temp .
15          MINUS {?temp time:intervalAfter ?interv .}
16      }""")
17
18 print"\n--- Last Interaction ---"
19 for row in qres:
20      service, interaction = row
21      s = service.rsplit("#", 2)[1]
22      i = interaction.rsplit("#", 2)[1]
23      print"The last interation is"+ s +"/" + i
```

Listing 4.14 Querying a service system to obtain information on interactions and roles

The idea behind the query is to find all the interactions that do not have the time:intervalAfter predicate. If an interaction does not have a successor, then it must be a final interaction.

4.3.3 External Data Source Queries

One of the most interesting features of the Semantic Web is the Linked Data cloud. It brings the capability to access and retrieve several structured web data sources using queries, and combine the results to build new content. We have added to our IM service instance information from external resources to make it richer. The information came from dbpedia.org.

The first step consists in revisiting our IM service instance to make annotations to external background knowledge. Listing 4.3 specified two new resources that are created by the interaction `IncidentLogging`:

- `lss-usdl:createsResource :IncidentID`
- `lss-usdl:createsResource :IncidentRecord`

Listing 4.15 show how to semantically annotate these two resources with concepts defined by the knowledge base DBpedia:

```
1  :IncidentID a dbpediar:Identifier ;
2      rdfs:label "Incident ID".
3
4  :IncidentReport a dbpediar:Report ;
5      rdfs:label"Report" .
```

Listing 4.15 Semantically annotating the IM service with DBpedia knowledge

The prefix `dbpediar` points to <http://dbpedia.org/resource/>.

To ease the access to DBpedia we used the Python SPARQL Endpoint interface SPARQLWrapper. This object allows to make a query against an arbitrary data source, offering an SPARQL interface to Python language.

Listing 4.16 shows how this can be achieved.

```
1  from rdflib import Namespace, Graph, RDF, URIRef, RDFS
2  from SPARQLWrapper import SPARQLWrapper, JSON
3
4  g = Graph()
5  g.parse("file:ITIL_IM_service.ttl", format='n3')
6  lss_usdl = Namespace("http://w3id.org/lss-usdl/v1#")
7
8  # Query the IM Service to get the dbpedia resources that were used
9  qres = g.query(
10     '''''PREFIX lss-usdl: <http://w3id.org/lss-usdl/v1#>
11     PREFIX dbpediar: <http://dbpedia.org/resource#>
12     SELECT DISTINCT ?resource ?interaction ?dbp_resource
13     WHERE {
14         ?lss lss-usdl:hasInteraction ?interaction .
15         ?interaction lss-usdl:createsResource ?resource .
16         ?resource a ?dbp_resource .
17     }""")
18
19 # Prepare the query template to access and retrieve dbpedia resource
        descriptions
```

```
20 # We will only retrieve the abstract
21 sparql = SPARQLWrapper("http://dbpedia.org/sparql")
22 q_start ='''''''SELECT DISTINCT ?abstract
23    WHERE {
24        <''''''
25 q_end ='''''''> dbpedia-owl:abstract ?abstract .
26        FILTER(langMatches(lang(?abstract),''EN''))
27    }'''''''
28
29 # Use the template to create queries for the resources retrieved
        from the IM Service instance
30 print"\n--- Fetch DBPedia Resource Abstracts ---"
31 for row in qres:
32    resource, interaction, dbp_resource = row
33    r = resource.rsplit("#", 2)[1]
34    i = interaction.rsplit("#", 2)[1]
35
36    q = q_start + dbp_resource + q_end
37
38    sparql.setQuery(q)
39    sparql.setReturnFormat(JSON)
40    results=sparql.query().convert()
41    for result in results["results"]["bindings"]:
42        print result["abstract"]["value"]
```

Listing 4.16 Resources

We start by querying the IM service to get the DBpedia resources that were used (lines 8–17). The list of resources is stored in the variable `qres`. To access and retrieve DBpedia information on these resources, we prepare a query template (lines 19–27). The template will enable to retrieve information from the abstract predicate. Finally, we iterate through the variable `qres` and for each resource we use the template to dynamically construct a new query to retrieve resource information from DBpedia.

References

1. Jan Van Bon, Arjen de Jong, and Axel Kolthof. *Foundations of IT Service Management based on ITIL.* Van Haren Publishing, 2007.
2. Kerstin Gerke, Jorge Cardoso, and Alexander Claus. Measuring the compliance of processes with reference models. In *17th International Conference on Cooperative Information Systems (CoopIS)*, Algarve, Portugal, 2009. Springer.
3. Martin Hepp. Goodrelations: An ontology for describing products and services offers on the web. In *Knowledge Engineering: Practice and Patterns*, pages 329–346. Springer, 2008.
4. OGC. *ITIL Service Operation.* ITIL Series. Stationery Office, 2007.

Chapter 5
Tools and Applications

The LSS-USDL model is an important contribution towards a better formalization and standardization of service system management. This chapter describes two software tools developed to demonstrate the model's applicability to real world usage. The applicability of the model was evaluated using three use cases found in the literature. Those use cases were previously modeled using service blueprinting, enabling to compare our findings with previous work, and, thus, achieving a higher level of confidence of the model's applicability.

5.1 Tool Support

Because the LSS-USDL model was developed not only for academic purposes, but also for real world usage, we need to build a bridge between the theoretical approach and the expected model usage. Therefore, we discuss two software tools we have developed that aim to show the applicability of our model for real world usage. Software tools for describing services are relatively rare. While we may find some examples for the e³ service model [1], none describe services using a white-box perspective. Therefore, the tools developed present an additional value to Service Science.

- The first tool is a LSS-USDL graphical editor. It intends to show that it is possible to express and model service systems using a simple graphical notation. It also intends to show that the proposed model is flexible and supports different service views.
- The second tool is a data converter to and from Linked USDL [2]. Data conversion is the process of converting computer data from one format to another. This not only demonstrates the model's ability to generate custom service descriptions, such as a customer-based description like Linked USDL, but also demonstrates an easy transition from service systems expressed in other models to LSS-USDL.

Both tools were bundled into one web application, because their features bring greater value when combined together.

© The Author(s) 2014
J. Cardoso et al., *Service Systems*,
SpringerBriefs in Computer Science, DOI 10.1007/978-3-319-10813-1_5

5.2 Graphical LSS-USDL Editor

The editor for LSS-USDL is a prototype that provides a graphical user interface that enables the modeling of service systems without the need to manually write RDF statements (as done in Chap. 3). This is an important proof of concept, not only because service systems are typically designed by managers and business owners whose technical skills do not usually embrace formal languages such as RDF, but also because service systems can easily reach high levels of complexity. Therefore, a good user interface for modeling is required to avoid high cognitive work and facilitate rapid data input.

Figure 5.1 shows the service blueprint view of the LSS-USDL editor.

The central feature of this tool is the management of service system instances according to the LSS-USDL model. A user may view, create, edit, or remove any element of a service system, including the service system itself.

5.2.1 The Concept of View

The tool was designed to illustrate the concept of view, meaning that the same service system can be observed and analyzed according to different service views.

In the example from Fig. 5.1, we have taken a blueprint view of a service system. The horizontal axis indicates the chronological sequence of interactions or activities and the vertical axis separates the different areas of actions [3]: line of interaction, line of visibility, and line of internal interaction. The line of visibility is also regarded

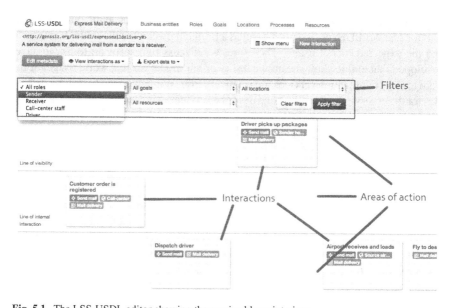

Fig. 5.1 The LSS-USDL editor showing the service blueprint view

Fig. 5.2 Service views

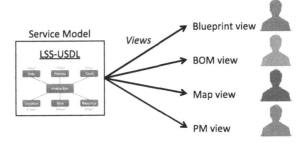

as the separation between the service "font stage" and "back stage" [4]. Since this is a well known method for service modeling, it is an important inspiration for our model. Hence, although our model is meant to work as an ontology for service systems, its graphical representation can work as an improved version of a service blueprinting.

When using the blueprint view, the visualization of a service system is centered on the flow of its interactions. This view highlights the temporal relations between them and divides them by areas of action. Other views are made available by the tool. We may also see interactions as a plain list and apply filters. These two different visualizations show that it is possible to provide meaningful views of a service system based on users' needs.

Other views that can be developed and should be explored in the future include (see Fig. 5.2):

BOM View A bill of materials (BOM) view provides a comprehensive list of the resources (see Chap. 3) required by a service system to operate. A BOM is usually represented in a hierarchical format, with the topmost level showing the end resource, and the bottom level displaying individual components and materials.

Map View The various interactions that occur during the provision of a service can be visualized using a map view, such as Google Maps, for visualizing interactions geographically. Metaphor visualizations, like a metro map, is an effective and simple method to convey complex insights by positioning information graphically to organize and structure it.

Project Management View Information on interaction points, temporal dependencies, and roles can be used to generate project management instructions for balancing cost and time requirements for different resources needed by a service. It supports human resource recruiting, people coordination, and tracking service delivery progresses against established plans.

5.2.2 Linked Data Integration

This tool also shows how a service system can be deeply integrated with the Linked Data Cloud using semantic enrichment. The importance of this integration was explained in Sect. 3.5. Hence, we may use it to connect LSS-USDL concepts

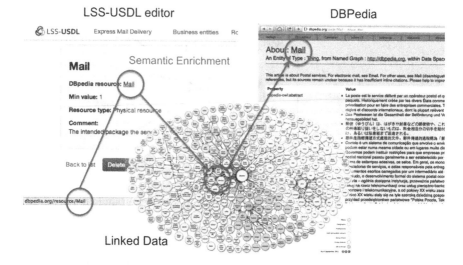

Fig. 5.3 Semantic enrichment: linking LSS-USDL concepts to DBPedia resources

to elements from external knowledge bases and ontologies as already explained. Figure 5.3 shows an example. The `Resource` element from LSS-USDL is connected to the DBpedia background knowledge from `DBpedia:mail`.

5.2.3 System Architecture

The application architecture follows an MVC (Model-View-Controller) approach, as depicted in Fig. 5.4. This means that when a user makes a request to the application, it is received by a router (1) that forwards it to the corresponding controller (2). The controller is where we may find the application logic. It then fetches the models it needs (3). A model is a data entity, such as a service system or an interaction. The

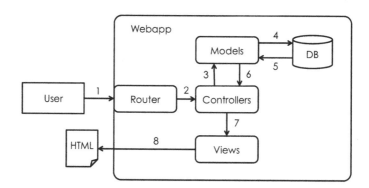

Fig. 5.4 Architecture of the LSS-USDL graphical editor tool

models are fetched from the database (4, 5) and returned to the controller (6). Finally, it returns the relevant view (7), which generates the HTML page that the user sees (8).

5.3 Linked USDL Import/Export Tool

The objective of developing an import/export tool was to make the LSS-USDL and Linked USDL (Unified Service Description Language) [5] models interoperable by enabling an automatic data conversion from one model to the other. This means that it should be possible to convert an LSS-USDL model into a corresponding Linked USDL model and vice versa. The challenges this objective creates are the non-trivial process of aligning the elements of two different models, exporting/importing data from one model to the another, and also the lack of existing service descriptions in Linked USDL. While LSS-USDL follows a white-box approach and describes external and internal elements of a service system, Linked USDL is technologically a similar model (it was implemented with Semantic Web technologies), but follows a black-box approach and describes only external (interface) details.

Linked USDL describes services in a comprehensive way by providing a business or commercial envelope around services [6]. Therefore, Linked USDL is seen has one of the foundational technologies for setting up emerging infrastructures for the Future Internet, web service ecosystems, and the Internet/web of services. Linked USDL was developed for describing business, software, or real-world services using computer-understandable specifications. It takes the form of a normalized schema which is an approach used in many fields to facilitate the exchange of data and integration of information systems.

While these two models do not share the same concepts, it is still possible to find common concepts (attributes) that enable a mapping between the two.

5.3.1 Model Mapping

While one of the objectives of data conversion is to maintain all of the data, and as much of the embedded information as possible, this can only be done if the target format supports the same features and data structures present in the source format. The conversion of an LSS-USDL to a Linked USDL instance, and vice versa, necessarily involves loss of information, because the set of characteristics (classes and properties) modeled by the two languages intersect but are not equal. Therefore, the mapping between LSS-USDL and Linked USDL, depicted in Table 5.1, was constructed.

5.3.2 System Architecture

Figure 5.5 depicts the architecture of this tool, integrated in the aforementioned graphical editor. When users' requests for an import or export operation reach the controller, the special model SemanticWorker is called. This model does not represent

Table 5.1 Mapping of
LSS-USDL concepts to
Linked USDL concepts

LSS-USDL	Linked USDL
Service system	Service
Customer interaction	Interaction point
Role	Interacting entity
Time	Time spanning entity
Resource	rdf:Resource
hasInteraction	hasInteractionPoint
isPerformedBy	hasInteractingEntity
hasTemporalEntity	spansInterval
receivesResource	receives
returnsResource	yields

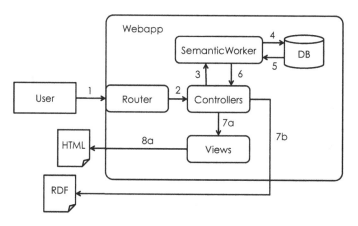

Fig. 5.5 Architecture of the Linked USDL export/import tool

any entity nor does it have a related database table. It does, however, interact with the database multiple times in order to create new entities from the provided RDF file or create a new semantic graph based on the existing entities. Its response (6) will be a confirmation for imports or a semantic graph for exports. If the user is importing a file, the controller will then call the view of the newly imported service system (7a) to be displayed to the user (8a). If the user is exporting a service system, the controller will return the exported RDF file (7b).

This tool acts as a proof of concept to show that it is possible to export an LSS-USDL service system model into different service descriptions and also to make use of existing service descriptions to rapidly build an LSS-USDL service model. This was added as a feature to the graphical editor because the two tools provide greater value when combined: it is possible to edit a service system by importing a Linked USDL specification and the export feature is now extended to support exporting both to an LSS-USDL or Linked USDL format.

5.4 Examples of Applications

Each of the following sections will introduce a different use case: express mail delivery, bookstore kiosk, and photo sharing webapp. Each one exemplifies how the LSS-USDL model and the LSS-USDL editor can be used in practice.

5.4.1 Express Mail Delivery

The first use case is an express mail delivery service system originally modeled to illustrate the features of a service blueprint [7]. The blueprint is depicted in Fig. 5.6.

Based on the service blueprint of the express mail delivery use case, we may build an RDF file with that information represented as an LSS-USDL service system. By inspecting the file (shown in Listing 5.1), we can see that the service system is fully described without losing the original information (considering that some slight adaptations were done for more cleanness). Furthermore, new data was added to enrich the system with context information, such as the resources in use and the location of each interaction.

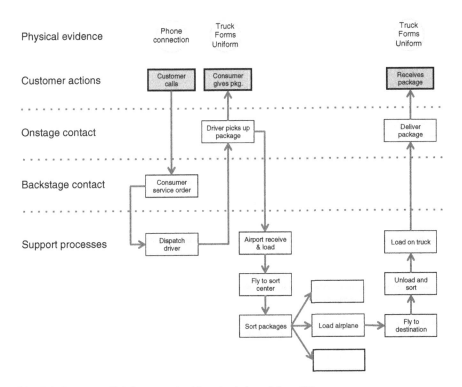

Fig. 5.6 Express mail delivery service blueprint (adapted from [7])

```
1   :Sender a lss-usdl:Role ;
2     rdfs:label "Sender" ;
3     rdfs:comment "The person/customer who intends to send a mail" .
4
5   :SendMail a lss-usdl:Goal ;
6     rdfs:label "Send mail" ;
7     rdfs:comment "To send an express mail" .
8
9   :SenderHome a lss-usdl:Location ;
10    rdfs:label "Sender home" ;
11    lss-usdl:isLocatedIn :SenderRegion .
12
13  :SenderData a lss-usdl:KnowledgeResource ;
14    rdfs:label "Sender data" ;
15    rdfs:comment "Name, address, etc. of sender" .
16
17  :ReceiverData a lss-usdl:KnowledgeResource ;
18    rdfs:label "Receiver data" ;
19    rdfs:comment "Name, address, etc. of receiver" .
20
21  :MailDelivery a lss-usdl:Process ;
22    rdfs:label "Mail delivery" .
23
24  :CustomerCallsTime a time:ProperInterval ;
25    time:intervalEquals :CustomerOrderIsRegisteredTime .
26
27  :CustomerCalls a lss-usdl:CustomerInteraction ;
28    rdfs:label "Customer calls" ;
29    lss-usdl:performedBy :Sender ;
30    lss-usdl:hasGoal :SendMail ;
31    lss-usdl:hasTime [
32      a lss-usdl:Time ;
33      lss-usdl:hasTemporalEntity :CustomerCallsTime
34    ] ;
35    lss-usdl:hasLocation :SenderHome ;
36    lss-usdl:belongsToProcess :MailDelivery ;
37    lss-usdl:receivesResource :SenderData ;
38    lss-usdl:receivesResource :ReceiverData .
```

Listing 5.1 Express mail delivery RDF extract

For the interaction `CustomerCalls`, we defined the role `Sender`, the goal `SendMail`, the location `SenderHome`, the process `MailDelivery`, and the two resources that the service system is receiving: `SenderData` and `ReceiverData`. We are also stating that this interaction is happening at the same time of the interaction `CustomerOrderIsRegistered`.

Now that we have the service model in RDF, we can import it to the graphical editor.[1] Figure 5.7 shows a screenshot of the result. This validates not only the correctness of that tool but also the graphical representation of the model.

---

[1] Result found in http://lss-usdl-editor.herokuapp.com/service_systems/5.

Fig. 5.7 Extended service blueprint of the express mail delivery use case

5.4.2 Bookstore Kiosk

In our second use case, we explored the example of a bookstore kiosk used by customers and employees to achieve their goals. Customers want to find and buy books, and employees want to manage stocks and identify book misplacements [8]. This use case is particularly interesting because it encompasses different goals from different stakeholders (customers and employees). Figures 5.8 and 5.9 depict the original service blueprint for the customer interactions and employee interactions, respectively.

We start by modeling the service system using the graphical editor to evaluate the usefulness of the editing tool and how it compares to modeling by writing the RDF statements[2] manually. Figure 5.10 shows a screenshot of the results. We can then export the service system to an RDF file and verify that we now have a valid LSS-USDL specification. This means that the tool can build service models and provide them in the semantic notation we desired.

This service system is more complex than the one in the previous use case. Using the graphical editor, however, greatly facilitates and accelerates its modeling. However, since this is a prototype, some interaction elements could be improved, such as mass-assigning common data to several interactions, which currently has to be done individually.

With the service model loaded by the editing tool it is possible to apply filters to get different views on the service system. We may apply a filter that shows the workflow for the customers interface (filtering by process "Customer interactions") and another filter that shows the workflow for the employees interface (filtering

_____

[2] Result found in http://lss-usdl-editor.herokuapp.com/service_systems/6.

Physical Evidence	Kiosk	Welcome Screen/ Members Card	Member Profile Screen	Member Profile/Search Interface	Book Directions/ Map, Coupon	Books	Books/Receipt
User Actions	Customer approaches bookstore kiosk	Customer swipes members card, logs in to kiosk	Customer considers suggestions	Customer searches for book	Customer prints book location map and coupon discounts	Customer walks to book locations and retrieves books	Customer discards one book and purchases the rest
Front Stage		Welcome screen	Members profile screen, suggestions, promotions	Kiosk search interface	Book location and tailored promotions		Checkout and registers
Back Stage		Kiosk software queries	Kiosk returns user profile, suggestions, promotions	Kiosk software queries, kiosk returns	Kiosk returns book location, bundled promotional discounts		Systems logs customer purchases
Support		Customer database	Marketing database	Inventory DB/ Location DB			Customer DB/ Inventory DB

Fig. 5.8   Customer interactions of the bookstore kiosk original service blueprint (adapted from [8])

Physical Evidence		Employee Dashboard	Employee Dashboard	Map/Book	Employee Dashboard	Employee Dashboard	Map/Books
User Actions	Employee checks computer screen	Employee sees zombie book action alert	Employee clicks on alert	Employee retrieves book and replaces it	Employee sees restocking action alert	Employee clicks on alert	Employee retrieves copies from stock and replenishes shelf
Front Stage		Employee dashboard alert section	Alert details link	Map with current book location	Employee dashboard alert section	Alert details link	Map with stock room and shelf book locations
Back Stage		Enterprise Service Use (ESB) integrates RFID data identifies zombie book	Employee system queries	Kiosk returns zombie books current location	ESB Integrates RFID data, identifies book that needs restocking	Employee system queries	Kiosk returns book's location in stock room and target shelf location
Support		Event Stream Processing (ESP), RFID Tracking tool, Inventory DB	Location DB		ESP, RFID Tracking tool, Inventory DB	Location DB	

Fig. 5.9   Employee interactions in the bookstore kiosk original service blueprint (adapted from [8])

Fig. 5.10 Extended service blueprint of the bookstore kiosk use case

by process "Employee interactions"). These two filters show the (adapted) service models found in [8].

The RDF statements for the customers interface workflow can be created by applying the aforementioned filter and selecting the option "Export filtered data to LSS-USDL file". The resulting file, which describes just a portion of the original service model, without many line breaks and comments, is larger than the file of the previous use case. The resulting file has now a valid LSS-USDL service model in a valid RDF notation.

This tool has the disadvantage of outputting RDF statements that lack the organization and comments that we saw in the previous use case. This may make the RDF statements harder to understand by humans. However, if readability is required, modeling the service system with this tool and after exporting reorganizing elements and commenting is still much faster than writing all the statements manually.

5.4.3 Photo Sharing Webapp

The third use case is a Software-as-a-Service (SaaS) webapp for sharing photos of travel destinations that was modeled as a service blueprint during a process of service design [9]. A service design process for a SaaS is a user-centric process that tries to better understand business and customer needs, and optimizes the service based on the analysis of interaction tasks. It is, therefore, a relevant use case to study in the context of our work. The original service blueprint is depicted in Fig. 5.11.

We have already showed the use of the LSS-USDL model, the graphical editor, and the import/export tool. We now focus on the Linked USDL converter tool. To do so, the interface of this service system was modeled in Linked USDL. Listing 5.2 shows the corresponding RDF statements.

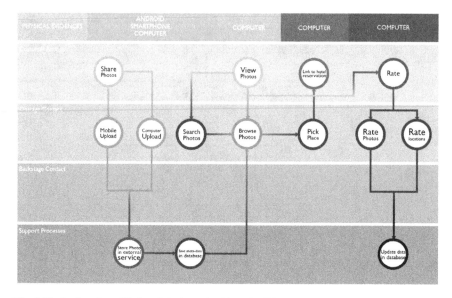

Fig. 5.11 SaaS webapp klinkr original service blueprint [9]

```
1   @prefix rdf: <http://www.w3.org/1999/02/22-rdf-syntax-ns#> .
2   @prefix rdfs: <http://www.w3.org/2000/01/rdf-schema#> .
3   @prefix time: <http://www.w3.org/2006/time#> .
4   @prefix xsd: <http://www.w3.org/2001/XMLSchema#> .
5   @prefix usdl: <http://www.linked-usdl.org/ns/usdl#> .
6   @prefix : <http://genssiz.dei.uc.pt/research/service-design/klinkr#> .
7
8   :Klinkr a usdl:Service ;
9     rdfs:label "klinkr" ;
10    rdfs:comment "klinkr is the new way to share photos of locations
            you've been to and to find amazing new locations to visit all
            around the globe." .
11
12  :User a usdl:InteractingEntity ;
13    rdfs:label "User" ;
14    rdfs:comment "Web and mobile user that submits and browses photos." ;
15    usdl:hasEntityType [
16      a usdl:Consumer
17    ] .
18
19  :Photo a rdf:Resource ;
20    rdfs:label "Photo" ;
21    rdfs:comment "Photo of a travelling site. Ideally, it should have
            geolocation metadata for easier identification of the
            locations." .
22
23  :HotelReservation a rdf:Resource ;
24    rdfs:label "Hotel reservation" ;
```

```
25   rdfs:comment "A reservation made through klinkr to a hotel near a
         travelling destination." .
26
27   :RatingInfo a rdf:Resource ;
28     rdfs:label "Rating info" ;
29     rdfs:comment "A rating that a user does to a photo or location." .
30
31   :SharePhotos a usdl:InteractionPoint ;
32     rdfs:label "Share photos" ;
33     rdfs:comment "Users can share photos of locations using the website
         or directly from their mobile phones." ;
34     usdl:receives :Photo ;
35     usdl:hasInteractingEntity :User .
36
37   :ViewPhotos a usdl:InteractionPoint ;
38     rdfs:label "View photos" ;
39     rdfs:comment "Users can browse the online catalogue of user-submited
         photos." ;
40     usdl:yields :Photo ;
41     usdl:hasInteractingEntity :User ;
42     usdl:spansInterval :ViewPhotosTime .
43
44   :ViewPhotosTime a time:ProperInterval .
45
46   :LinkToHotelReservation a usdl:InteractionPoint ;
47     rdfs:label "Link to hotel reservation" ;
48     rdfs:comment "Users can make a hotel reservation for a travelling
         destination when viewing photos of that destination." ;
49     usdl:yields :HotelReservation ;
50     usdl:hasInteractingEntity :User ;
51     usdl:spansInterval :LinkToHotelReservationTime .
52
53   :LinkToHotelReservationTime a time:ProperInterval ;
54     time:intervalAfter :ViewPhotosTime .
55
56   :Rate a usdl:InteractionPoint ;
57     rdfs:label "Rate" ;
58     rdfs:comment "Users can rate photos and locations to help filtering
         the best content." ;
59     usdl:receives :RatingInfo ;
60     usdl:hasInteractingEntity :User ;
61     usdl:spansInterval :RateInterval .
62
63   :RateTime a time:ProperInterval ;
64     time:intervalAfter :ViewPhotosTime .
```

Listing 5.2 Photo sharing webapp RDF statements for Linked USDL description

This file was then imported into the graphical editor.[3] Figure 5.12 shows a screen-shot of the result.

Note that this service system is incomplete because it was generated from a Linked USDL description. Since Linked USDL is a service description language

---

[3] Result found in http://lss-usdl-editor.herokuapp.com/service_systems/7.

Fig. 5.12 Extended service blueprint of the SaaS webapp use case

for customer interactions, all the service interactions that happen in the other areas of action (i.e., inside the black box) are omitted. Moreover, Linked USDL does not include concepts such as goals or interaction locations. Therefore, those elements will be missing when mappings from Linked USDL to LSS-USDL.

This means that the resulting LSS-USDL service model will generally lack completeness. However, after this first automatic generation, it is possible to add the missing information. Hence, such a tool can be seen as a quick start for modeling service systems in LSS-USDL from Linked USDL. We can now export the generated service model into a LSS-USDL specification.

References

1. Sybren Kinderen and Jaap Gordijn. Reasoning about substitute choices and preference ordering in e-services. In *Advanced Information Systems Engineering*, pages 390–404. Springer, 2008.
2. Jorge Cardoso, Carlos Pedrinaci, Torsten Leidig, Paulo Rupino, and Peter De Leenheer. Open semantic service networks. In *International Symposium on Services Science (ISSS), Leipzig, Germany*, 2012.
3. Sabine Fließ and Michael Kleinaltenkamp. Blueprinting the service company: Managing service processes efficiently. *Journal of Business Research*, 57(4):392–404, 2004.
4. Robert Glushko and Lindsay Tabas. Designing service systems by bridging the front stage and back stage. *Information Systems and e-Business Management*, 7:407–427, 2009.
5. Carlos Pedrinaci, Jorge Cardoso, and Torsten Leidig. Linked USDL: A Vocabulary for Web-scale Service Trading. In *11th Extended Semantic Web Conference*, Crete, Greece, May 2014.
6. Jorge Cardoso, Alistair Barros, Norman May, and Uwe Kylau. Towards a unified service description language for the internet of services: Requirements and first developments. In *Services Computing (SCC), 2010 IEEE International Conference on*, pages 602–609. IEEE, 2010.
7. Dwayne Gremler. Service Blueprinting: Designing Service from the Customer's Point of View. In *Phonak Practice Development Conference*, 2011.
8. Robert Glushko. Seven contexts for service system design. *Handbook of service science*, pages 219–249, 2010.

9. Ricardo Lopes, João Duro, Rui Chicória, Ana Mateus, and Pedro Raposeira. klinkr - Using COnCoRD: A Customer Centered Service Design Approach. http://eden.dei.uc.pt/jcardoso/Services/Concord/Klinkr-Service-Design-Using-CONCORD.pdf, 2012.

Chapter 6
Conclusions

This chapter summarizes the approach we have followed to develop a model to represent service systems. It also discusses our findings and describes how this work may benefit our society.

6.1 Summary

The main goal of this research was to conceive a model for describing service systems using a white-box approach and using a computer-understandable language. Such an approach sets the grounds to enable the execution of automated tasks such as service simulation, service analytics, and the service compliance analysis of service systems.

We discussed and analyzed several models for representing service systems. Those models, however, did not produce computer-understandable information or did not adopted a white-box approach, thus, they were not capable of fulfilling our initial goal. However, their study enabled to identify the most common service system concepts (attributes) found in the literature.

Building upon the aforementioned concepts and the journalism interrogative pronouns, we were able to characterize a service system as a flow of service interactions and create the 6-point interaction star model.

The model was implemented using Semantic Web technologies and included external vocabularies from the Linked Data Cloud. We have chosen to name it Linked Service System for USDL (LSS-USDL) because it builds upon the research efforts of the Linked USDL model and because it uses Linked Data principles for modeling. It was constructed using RDF and its specification is freely available at http://w3id. org/lss-usdl/v1. Examples are available at https://github.com/rplopes/lss-usdl. Both are governed by the Creative Commons Attribution 3.0 Unported License.[1]

---

[1] http://creativecommons.org/licenses/by/3.0.

© The Author(s) 2014   89
J. Cardoso et al., *Service Systems*,
SpringerBriefs in Computer Science, DOI 10.1007/978-3-319-10813-1_6

6.2 Tooling

In order to demonstrate the applicability of the model, two prototype software tools were developed. The first tool was a graphical editor that provided easier and faster modeling capabilities. The second tool was a converter to and from Linked USDL to ease migrations between different service description languages. These two tools were bundled in a webapp that was deployed online at http://lss-usdl-editor. herokuapp.com. The code is freely available at https://github.com/rplopes/lss-usdl_ editor under the same license as the LSS-USDL model.

To evaluate this model, we studied three different use cases (express mail delivery, bookstore kiosk, and photo sharing webapp) and discussed the results.

6.3 Implication for Society

While the services sector is the most influential economic sector of modern society [1–3], it is still the sector with less scientific understanding [4]. The LSS-USDL model is, thus, a proposal to enable a much needed understanding of this dominant economic sector.

Having a tool that enables modeling service systems brings many advantages, which include:

Open Services Governments, and organizations in general, can make their service systems open to third parties and citizens to foster their reuse and continuous improvement via crowdsourced initiatives. For governments, transparency can incentive citizens to participate in the improvements of services and working procedures.

Service Analytics A formal representation of service systems enables to conduct service analytics to better understand how services operate and how they might benefit from improvement.

Business-to-Business Integration B2B integration has mainly been achieved by using business protocols to bridge companies at the data and process levels. Forms, such as purchasing orders, are encoded with standard protocols, and exchanged among industry partners. With LSS-USDL this integration goes to the next level, the service level.

Service Search Since LSS-USDL provides a detailed description of services' interactions, end-users can achieve a higher precision and recall during their search for services. Service composition can be archived taking into account physical locations, goals, and temporal information.

The potential of the LSS-USDL model is very attractive and aligned with recent initiates such as Open Data and Open Innovation. In fact, it is a catalyst for the Semantic Web and Linked Data, which so far have been mainly available for passive information retrieval [5].

References

1. Jorge Cardoso, Alistair Barros, Norman May, and Uwe Kylau. Towards a unified service description language for the internet of services: Requirements and first developments. In Services Computing (SCC), 2010 IEEE International Conference on, pages 602–609. IEEE, 2010.
2. Holger Luczak, Christian Gill, and Bernhard Sander. Architecture for Service Engineering The Design and Development of Industrial Service Work. In Dieter Spath and Klaus-Peter Fähnrich, editors, Advances in Services Innovations, pages 47–63. Springer, Berlin Heidelberg, 2007.
3. Jim Spohrer, Paul Maglio, John Bailey, and Daniel Gruhl. Steps toward a science of service systems. Computer, 40(1):71–77, 2007.
4. Henry Chesbrough and Jim Spohrer. A research manifesto for services science. Communications of the ACM, 49(7):35–40, 2006.
5. Barry Norton, Reto Krummenacher, Adrian Marte, and Dieter Fensel. Dynamic linked data via linked open services. In Workshop on Linked Data in the Future Internet at the Future Internet Assembly, pages 1–10, 2010.

Index

© The Author(s) 2014
J. Cardoso et al., *Service Systems*,
SpringerBriefs in Computer Science, DOI 10.1007/978-3-319-10813-1